LOW MAGIC

I

Witchcraft

TEN years ago we should have begun this chapter by saying that Witchcraft was the collection of the practices of Low Magic long worn out and which were like the slime at the bottom of the Lake of Occult Sciences, at the present day decanted by the wisdom of the elect. But after reading this or that formulary or ritual of Eliphas Levi, of Papus or of Pierre Piobb, or some volume of Jagot, all of which deal quite seriously of these extraordinary matters, after learning that phenomena like those of psychometry or clairvoyance by mirrors are scientifically obtained, and that some queer act of bewitching does not belong to the realm of chimeras, we are compelled to stop on the threshold of the mysterious Temple on the other side of which we merely imagined a collection of illusions or cheatings, and we open the door only with caution to see and try to understand.

Very imprudent would be the man, who, without prejudice, and anxious to make no errors, would dive for information into some History of Occult Sciences like that of the Count de Resi, or even the greater number of the contemporary books which claim that they are free " from the superstition of former times." Let us, objectively and without comment for the moment, confine ourselves to remarking that witchcraft goes back to the very oldest times, and is merged with Magic, which accounts for the name of magicians given indiscriminately to sorcerers and to magi.

The Jews, the Greeks, the Romans, the Germans, the Scandinavians practised Witchcraft, but it must be noted that a time came when they distinguished between Magi and Sorcerers, and punished the latter as criminals. The same thing happened in the Middle Ages when they were confounded with Heretics. The fight of Justice against them relaxed in the 15th century, when an era of free discussion seemed to dawn. But Papal Bulls [1] soon reinforced the horrors

---

[1] Innocent VIII (1484), Alexander VI, Leo X, John XIII. The rising Protestantism added to the fury of the Church, which engulfed Protestants and Witches in one debauch of cruel punishments.

of the Inquisition. The fires of persecution multiplied, again exciting the people. Under Charles IX there were more than 30,000 witches in France.

. . . . . .

Let us now mention the " crimes " of the witches, catalogued by Bodin under fifteen main heads. And first let us mention the Sabbath, which in reality was the ceremony of initiation, and the origin of which seems to go back to the earliest days of Christianity, when the Celts, in protest against the new religion, secretly preserved the worship of the god Pan and celebrated it according to a ritual which was modified from time to time and eventually came to follow the rites of the adepts of Satanism. [1]

The Great Sabbath united once in three months all the sorcerers and witches of a State. The Little Sabbath called together once a week the initiates of a town or small region. It took place in a lonely spot, a wood, ruins, the side of a lake, cross roads (even if a cross was erected there), the foot of a gallows, and began towards midnight. The initiates arrived riding on broomsticks, and very soon the Devil in person (was it trickery, hallucination or evocation ?) was seated on a throne, having at his side the Queen-Mother, or Queen of Witches. Sometimes a Goat took the place of the Devil. And before the All-Lowest, either in the flesh or by deputy, the new recruits were brought.

And now the neophyte prostrates himself, renounces God, the Virgin, the Catholic Faith, delivers himself body and soul to Lucifer, and takes the oath of allegiance to him. Then he kisses his left hand, his mouth, his heart and his genitals. The Black Master places the *stigma diaboli* on his left shoulder. After this the assistants strip him and rub him with a fœtid ointment. [2]

Thereupon homage is rendered to Lucifer by kissing his base, and work begins. Powders, drinks, magic ointments are prepared, using mainly among plants ivy and hemlock, valerian and asphodel, and also extraordinary ingredients such as snakes' teeth, toad's skin, the entrails of hanged men, the brain of a newborn babe, the excrement of the owl, the gall of the goat, in short everything that may seem strange, repugnant, horrible. Spells are uttered, bewitchments made, curses pronounced. Then the festival begins. Scenes of extravagant eroticism take place, wild dances are performed in a fury of exaltation which turns all heads and ends in a kind of general epilepsy and in monstrous connections. But fatigue and exhaustion in the end overcome the victims, they collapse until, when the sound of infernal music

[1] Michelet thinks that possibly Witchcraft was in some way a revolt of the people against the double power of the Church and the State.

[2] It may also be that having first been rubbed with this ointment, the adepts went to the Sabbath *in a dream*, or with their *astral body* (see Appendix).

restores their vigour, the celebrated Round of the Sabbath begins, which ends at cock-crow in a general flight.

About the year 1300 a supplemental ritual began to be used, the Black Mass. It started with the general confession, in which of course every one boasted of the most abominable crimes. Satan or his deputy then read a blasphemous parody of the ordinary Mass, preached a sermon inciting to evil, ridiculed in gestures frequently indecent the consecration, gave in communion to his disciples no one knows what fantastic meats and drinks (even the remains of deceased sorcerers), and then gave free course to the above mentioned convulsions.

The frequently sadistic imagination of the judges was never at a loss in order to obtain confessions from those accused of witchcraft and subsequently executing them. It was by the cleansing (!) fire that they were chastised after trials abounding in judicial infamies as to which we shall keep silence.

These trials were especially numerous in the 16th century which saw the condemnation amongst others of Verdun and Burgot who confessed having turned themselves into wolves and devoured children, the famous sorcerer Trois-Echelles who claimed to have 3,000 accomplices, Gilles Garnier of Lyons, accused of lycanthropy and anthropophagy, 400 Huguenots at one time who were charged with magic as a convenient means of punishing their heresy, La Mole and Coconas who, it was said, tried to bewitch Henri III, and a considerable number of other " apostates, idolaters, sodomites, homicides, enchanters and worshippers of the Devil."

" The examination in these strange trials," writes Florian Parmentier, " presented inexplicable anomalies. Nothing could shake the conviction of the judges, neither the conflicting depositions of the witnesses nor the absurd tales of the accused. Further not one minute of judgment specifies the actual offence."

We are entitled to conclude on the one hand that the abominations of the sorcerers and witches have been enormously exaggerated, and on the other hand that in the case of most of them there existed, in the words of Dr. Regnard, " an epidemic disease of the mind " which brought on all the above mentioned exaltations, some of which may have degenerated into the fiercest eroticism as well as into actual murders.

.   .   .   .   .   .

In the opinion of Lombroso (*Hypnotism and Spiritism*), the primitives, the ignorant country people worshipped individuals (sorcerers, magicians, prophets) who were true mediums, believed to be capable (and sometimes actually capable) of breaking the laws of nature by seeing at a distance, prophesying, levitating, communicating with angels, devils, and especially with the dead.

In Sicily the people believe that men possessed have the gift of tongues, that witches transform themselves into cats, into bats, make women barren, cast spells, etc., that there are good and bad Ladies of the Night. In Benevento Blasio has seen as many as one per cent. of the population hysterical, alcoholic, epileptic, and speaking a jargon of their own.

In Portugal witches grew rich from predictions and philters. According to Maurerie, they had their own quarter in Lisbon, and the police tried in vain to take proceedings.

In France Brittany and the Vosges were especially infested by magicians who told the future and cast spells. Looked at closely, the majority of these persons only produced more or less efficiently most of the hyperpsychic phenomena which to-day are well known (see Third Part).

The Arabs have their aissaouas, their dervishes expert in clairvoyance by means of the magic mirror, the crystal or water, their convulsed medidubs. The Patagonians have their prophet-physicians, who, as in Brazil, are almost always epileptics. The Kaffirs have isangonas or diviners who have to go through an apprenticeship. The sorcerers of Madagascar stand in the front rank.

There is no end to the list of the various sorcerers of the successive centuries and the various latitudes. But special mention is due to the Fakirs of India of whom a former Consul in Benares, Jacolliot, was one of the first to relate the marvellous feats. Thus the Fakir Covindaswamy, to name but one, was able, by leaning on the knob of a stick, to rise in the air with legs crossed in Eastern fashion and to remain in this position for twenty minutes, to make it impossible for any one to lift a small table which he had magnetised by laying his hands on it, to play a musical instrument from a considerable distance, to make a stick write, without his touching it, on the sand a word thought by another person, to make a papaw seed germinate and grow to eight inches by the laying on of hands, to let himself be put into a coffin and buried in the ground for ten months without dying, to produce above a chafing dish hands which move and pick flowers. All these phenomena belong clearly to mediumship or hyperpsychics (see Third Part).

. . . . . .

In his book on Witchcraft Mr. Florian Parmentier tries to take its mechanism to pieces, and says some very apt things about it, the chief of which is as follows :—

" The origin of the demoniac part of Witchcraft," he thinks, " comes in truth from the Catholic dogma relating to the existence of the Devil. Witchcraft has taken hold of this thought (which perhaps is but a symbol) and has made it into a reality which, in its turn deformed by the popular imagination, has become a new dogma, viz., the belief in a Devil having well settled shape and attributes (horns, cloven foot, tail, smell of sulphur, etc.), able to appear and disappear, full of an evil power and in short only desiring to do mischief. With whose assistance shall he do mischief? With whose but that of the sorcerers?

"On the other hand, the people, unable to explain the ills under which it laboured, found it only natural to attribute them to the Devil and to his agents. At once, then, sudden deaths, epilepsies and any illness out of the ordinary, accidents, reverses of fortunes, murrains, calamities of all kinds were attributed to sorcerers. Better still, or rather worse still, the fact of being independent, of having opinions contrary to those of the rest, knowing the properties of herbs and simples, being able to reduce a sprain, all this meant to be more or less in touch with the Devil. During a thousand years, says Michelet, the witch was the sole physician of the People. The wealthy had ercourse to certain rare men who were thought to be able to heal without recourse to witchcraft. But the *vulgum pecus* always applied to the *saga*, vague wise woman, or rather woman who was more or less a witch; out of respect she was called Good Lady; at bottom she inspired fear; further this healer did not hesitate to bring about abortions or poisonings which Medicine, then rudimentary, was unable to denounce (for autopsy was unknown).

"Besides," says Mr. Florian Parmentier very aptly, "since it was a religious dogma to believe in the Devil, why should it not be allowed to accuse him of everything which seemed supernatural? Thus we may explain the credulity of superior minds at the same time good Catholics, such as Pica della Mirandola, Jean Fernel or Ambrose Paré."

Finally his conclusion is well worth remembering :—"Luminosity, electro-magnetic waves, forces in motion and actions at the beginning of their performance, all these in the universe in fact repulse and attract each other and give rise to unsuspected reactions. Hypnotism, mental automatism, thought transference, opaque vision, high frequency electricity with its millions of oscillations per second, X rays and the photography of the Invisible, the telegraphing of pictures, tele-autography and tele-mechanics, the N ray and the emanations of radium, all these are so many forces which to-day are disciplined, phenomena which we know to be produced by radiation and to act at a distance on appropriate receivers. Now the human brain and the human nervous system are so far as we know the most perfected receiving apparatus for all magnetic currents, for all the vibrations of the psychic atmosphere. And this leads us to think in the last resort that manifestations attributed to occult causes have in truth merely changed their name, and that the witchcraft of the devil has been followed in our own time, the great scientific witchcraft which, like the other, has its initiations, its phenomena, its mysteries, its conquests of the infinite, and also its superstitions, its trickeries and its errors."

Where, however, Mr. Florian Parmentier makes a mistake, and where he goes farther than he needs for his exposition, is in saying that there is no call, in his opinion, to be surprised at the credulity of yesterday when we consider the credulity of to-day. Why, he asks in substance, in the 16th century should not people believe in the devil when in the 20th century they still believe in the follies of Spiritualism ! On the face of it he is right. As an occultist he exaggerates. There is no need to put in issue the disturbing although still unexplained phenomena of mediumship ; he thinks these are *natural* if they exist, and we agree with him on this point, for these phenomena do in truth come within the scope of natural events, since they are true and not chimerical. As to Spiritualism, he is perhaps somewhat hasty in condemning it.

Where he frankly is right is in seeking out and showing up the amount of imposture and charlatanism which exist in witchcraft. With him we are convinced that there were at the time thousands of tricks, that the judges proceeded through stupidity, through sadism and even through self-interest (they profited to some extent from the confiscation of the property of the condemned), that Witchcraft supported revolts against the Government, that crooks of all kinds used it for their own benefit (and also cunning lovers), that eroticism profited by it at a time when the law was severe with free love, that some so-called magic formulæ were at bottom mere aphrodisiacs, that hysteria played a considerable part in those troublous times when, in default of morphia or cocaine, the properties of opium, of stramonium, of belladonna, of datura, of hemp were brought into use, that the drugs prepared in accordance with magical formulæ must of necessity produce a thousand hallucinations, somnambulism, even the mad imaginings which caused sorcerers and witches to confess " crimes " which they had never committed except in dream, that hypnotism played its part in the matter (impressionability being greater than to-day and the number of neurotics and weaklings more considerable), that the spells cast might well be nothing but suggestion, that the cases of demoniac possession might be merely auto-suggestion (the same remark applying to exorcism), that sorcerers might be able, like some moderns, to heal or relieve through magnetism and to hypnotise themselves like the Fakirs, believe themselves, like the mediums, to be visited by spirits, and to practise witchcraft in the manner of Mr. de Rochas, by explaining this true phenomenon by the exteriorisation of sensitiveness.

Yes, we believe all that, and it considerably lessens the mysteries of Low Magic and makes them into a frequently caricaturing introduction to the great modern psychic experiments.

II

The Storehouse and the Prescriptions of Low Magic

After this preamble it will be surmised that we shall not occupy ourselves for long with the practices of Witchcraft. We shall give a list of them, together with the strange prescriptions and the grotesque storehouse of Low Magic, intentionally confusing the ancient and the mediæval tradition, and confining ourselves to extracting from curious books and spell-books of all kinds, which had an amazing circulation and which are still being republished and modernised, those things which appeared to us the least extravagant and also the most typical, all this, of course, merely as historical and informative. But those who in spite of everything think that these formulæ may possibly have retained some efficacy need not hesitate to try them.

It will not be difficult to find in the following information on any desired subject concerning these survivals from ancient times and popular beliefs, and we also mention the names and give some details of the most famous of the books of Ancient Magic. After that we shall go on to the *modernisation of traditional Magic.*

Abraxas

This first word correctly describes the storehouse of the sorcerers, the main items of which were natural talismans, magic formulæ, rings, wands, weapons, magic rings and mirrors, the flying pistol, baby's skins, virgin parchment, virgin wax and soil, etc.

The chief natural Talismans were :—

> The mandragora, inspiration of love.
> The topaz, driver off of black thoughts.
> The ruby, quieter of excited senses.
> The hyena skin, which makes invulnerable.
> Powdered toad, which produces love.
> The bezoar, universal panacea.

. . . . . .

Amulets and Talismans

These are various articles, consecrated or not, which protect against illness, misfortune and accident. They also bring luck and success. But, says E. Bosc, they are of value only if the wearer has faith in them. And Eliphas Levi says, " The talismans in this resemble the Catholic host, which is salvation for the just and damnation for the sinner, and which thus, according to the state of him who receives them, means God or the Devil."

The Jews have among their talismans a roll of parchment called *mezuroth*. They place it in the lintel of the doors of their houses, or carry it on them in a small case so as to comply with the saying in *Deuteronomy*, " You shall never forget the law of God and shall engrave it on the lintels of your doors."

The talismans sold by the pedlars of Occultism, or which are advertised, are swindles, says Schwaeble in his *Book of Luck*, seeing that, to be efficacious, the talisman must be made by the person it concerns. There are some which are worn on the person because they remedy one's defects or strengthen one's qualities, and others are used on special occasions only. Some writers say that for the former a metal disc must be cut corresponding to the planet which rules one's life, and the signs of such planet engraved on the disc ; others say that two discs must be used, one for the planet ruling one's life, the other for the planet strengthening or modifying it.

The following are also mentioned as bringing luck :—

A horn made of coral or gold or stone.

A piece of the cord of a hanged man.

One of the sacred stones in astrological relation with the wearer (see below).

A little bag containing the eye of a woodpecker, the eye of a weasel, a crystal ring, a penny with a hole in it, a fragment of an aerolith (stone fallen from the sky) and dust from a menhir.

Also a four-leaved clover, but picked by the wearer, either at midnight on a Friday during the first three days of the Moon, or in bright sunshine between noon and three o'clock either in a lonely spot or in a graveyard ; if it has not been picked by you yourself, it should be given you by a friend and handed to you by the stalk. Wear it round the neck in a locket.

Let us look at the *Jewish Kabbala* of Paul Vulliaud. Amulets, he says, are of great interest in the study of religions, of folklore, of practical Kabbala. Their use is universal, whether they are called Hemelets (in Persia), Amuleta (in Rome), Teraphim (in Mesopotamia), Phylacteries (in Greece), Totapoth (in Egypt), or Tebhulim (in Chaldea),

LOW MAGIC

Talismanic art is the art of making these articles from which we expect a *protection*, and the name of which means " that which is attached."

The first human ornaments seem to have been amulets (earrings, etc.) Breast jewelry, rings on the hand were charms. Precious stones were always looked upon as endowed with magic virtues. Soon the word amulet came to mean a small bag hung round the neck and containing roots, seeds and other articles which had an efficacious occult power, or a metal disc engraved with Kabbalistic signs.

The Jews had a whole series of forbidden and permitted amulets. A whole book might be written on their talismanic art, also on that of other nations. We shall forbear, merely saying that Christianity had and has its amulets (scapularies, medals, holy relics, etc.), the same as other religions. [1]

In conclusion let us draw attention to the theory and the instances of talismans given by Papus. [2]

The language of the Invisible World is the Picture, says the great modern magician, for the picture is understood by every one. Hence a symbolic language seen by clairvoyants, consecrated by Tradition and used in the making of talismans.

Talismans influence the plane which is in relation with the graphic characters of which they are made and with the ceremonies which have been used to fix their astral attraction.

The hieroglyphic signs of the talismans must be inscribed on virgin parchment on which no other image has yet been set, even in thought (what we have said above as to psychometry and as to objects retaining the impression of the persons and the things with which they have been in touch, will be remembered). Virgin parchment is made of the skin of still-born animals.

Magic Rings

These are amulets with varying properties according to their consecration. With their aid the magicians, it seems, worked miracles.

---

[1] The talismans used in magic are the visible signs of the Principles, the channels of energy, corresponding to piers ; they are the piers, the accumulators of the astral ; the energy is captured, imprisoned in them, directed by means of the *operations of the Magician*, through his incantations, the power of the strength of the Magician and the power borrowed by him from Nature, this energy being communicated to the things which are the conductors of the nervous and magneto-ethero-electric fluid.

The religious medals of all cults, the rosaries, the fetishes, the luck bringers, especially if in metal, the scapularies, are magic talismans. But the devout do not know the reason of their influence, they attribute it to the gods instead of referring it to the universal Energy, specialised by religious or purely magic rites (as the case may be), which rites still further increase the power of the talisman or the ceremony by reason of the Tradition (an occult chain in Space and Time) and the solidarity of the spirits all tending in the same direction and towards the same end. (Jollivet-Castelot).

[2] In the *Book of Luck*.

According to Ch. V. Langlois, there were two well defined kinds of magic rings :—

1. Those which gave their wearers supernatural powers.
2. Those which bound their wearers to some bondage.

One of the most famous rings of Antiquity was that called Solomon's ring in the stone of which the great King saw everything he wanted to know (this was no doubt a case of *clairvoyance* of which phenomenon we have already spoken).

The best known kinds of these rings were the following :—

The stellar rings which were worn, not on the finger, but round the neck like a scapulary.

The travellers' rings which enabled them to cover long distances without fatigue (there is no doubt that, through auto-suggestion, they simply doubled the energy of the traveller).

The rings of invisibility, like that of Gyges, King of Lydia, which made their wearer invisible to the eye. It had to be made of solid mercury and ornamented with a stone which is only found in the nest of the hoopoe.

It may be pointed out that wedding rings are a remnant of the magic rings. They are worn on the ring finger, because in chiromancy that finger corresponds to the heart. The husband will be master in the home, if, on placing it on his wife's finger, he is careful to push it right down.

Magic Weapons.

Everyone knows the marvels worked by the celebrated *Durandal,* the sword of Roland, who used to cleave a rock with it. It obviously was enchanted.

In witchcraft a magic or enchanted sword is an ordinary sword consecrated. The magic sword is used either to trace the magic circle, or in defence against the evil spirits of Invisibility.

A magic knife was a knife with a white handle, dipped in the blood of a male goose on the day and at the hour of Mercury in an increasing moon. Three ordinary Masses were read over this sword and certain mysterious signs were written on it in exorcised sulphuret of mercury.

Magical and Divining Rods

The practice of Rhabdomancy (divination by a rod) was one of the most highly honoured in Magic. It survives in the very remarkable art of the dowsers.

LOW MAGIC

According to Father Lebrun, a divining rod is made half of alder-wood, half of other wood. It is balanced on a pivot fixed in the earth in a spot where water may be expected to be. He says that before the sun has dispersed the morning dew, the alder, more porous than other wood, absorbs the aqueous emanations of the soil (sign of water) and dips down if there is a sheet of water or a spring. Nothing remains but to dig.

The celebrated rod with which Moses smote the rock to make water gush forth was undoubtedly a rod of this kind which he knew how to use.

Another kind of dowser's rod is simply a fork of walnut wood about 18 inches long, one year old and as thick as a finger. The rod is grasped by its two ends, the point of the fork forward, and the dowser goes slowly over the region where he expects to find water below ground. At the exact spot where there is water, the point of the rod dips towards the ground.

The rhabdomancer Royer used for this fork alder, oak or pear wood indiscriminately, balanced it on the back of his hands, and, walking slowly, pointed out where there was water at the moment when the rod began to turn by itself.

As will be seen, Rhabdomancy has nothing magical, and belongs to pure physics. But the ignorant are surprised by the phenomenon, and from surprise to a belief in witchcraft is but a step.

The true divining rod was used for three different discoveries—water, hidden metal, the track of man. This last named property is said to have been brought to light following on a very curious happening in Lyons which we shall briefly relate, for it was much discussed at the time, and has to some extent become classic in argument.

On the 5th July, 1692, in Lyons, a family of wine merchants were killed in their cellar with a bill-hook, and the money in the shop was stolen. In order to trace the murderers, a peasant of the Dauphiné, Jacques Aymar, was called in, as he was said to be able to follow the track of evildoers by means of a magic rod. The good man asked to be taken to the cellar, and although he had not been told anything, his rod began to turn in the exact two spots where the man and the woman had been killed. He himself became highly feverish ; he went back to the shop, and from there passed into the street, still led by his rod. He left the town, went along the right of the river, into the house of a gardener, maintained that the murderers must have sat down at his table to drink a bottle, which fact was confirmed by two children who were questioned and whom the rod had pointed out as knowing something of the drama. On the other hand, the authorities having buried in some land belonging to Mr. de Mongirol the bill-hook with which the crime had been committed, together with some others, Aymar found the former. Then he was accompanied by a Clerk of the Court and some archers. He went back to the Rhone and found that the culprits had taken a boat. Aymar followed them on the water as on the land, landed everywhere where they had landed, found the beds where they had slept, the tables where they had eaten. The magician in this way went as far as Beaucaire, knew that they had separated there, and followed the track of the accomplice who most strongly affected the rod. He went as far as a prison, and among a dozen prisoners, pointed to a hunchback who had been locked up an hour before for some petty theft. On being questioned, the man confessed after some resistance that he had been a witness of the crime committed by two others. Aymar starts off again, goes as far as Toulon and does not stop till he reaches the sea, where he says that the murderers have taken a boat to escape abroad.

That is the story. A treatise on the Divining Rod in two volumes[1] gives the following explanation :—

The Rod, also called Caduceus, divining Rod, Rod of Aaron, Staff of Jacob, etc., was known in all times, and many writers mention it. Its action is revealed by the " philosophy of corpuscles," the latter being volatile agents, subtle forms of matter which are capable of detaching themselves from bodies ; it is they which, escaping from the subterranean water, from a hidden treasure, or from a man whose track is followed, influence the divining rod, just as would happen in the case of the emanations of a scented object revealing its passage to those who did not see it ; the author likewise quotes the smell of dogs who follow or find their master, and he sees an analogy with the action of the rod, the latter being equally sensitive " to the corpuscles." But he admits that this sensitiveness belongs to the man who communicates it to his tool which without him, would remain inactive. And here he brings in the idea of magnetism.

As to the discovery of treasures, according to the author it must be assumed that the rod correctly handled is sensitive to metallic emanations, and he gives a list of mines found by this means, notably in the Pyrenees, the Languedoc, Auvergne, etc. He also describes the " face of the sky " under which the rod must be cut so as to find the mines in accordance with the metal which they contain.

It is very curious to discover from this little book the progress of criticism. Formerly the working of the rod was looked upon as demoniac. Here occult physics are brought in and the theory of corpuscles is discussed. Thus we attain to truth and the purely scientific explanations given for instance to the divining rod of the dowser, and which will some day in like manner be given of the other phenomena of rhabdomancy.

[1] *Occult Physics*, published by Moetiens at the Hague in 1772.

LOW MAGIC

Enchiridion

The *Enchiridion* is a collection of magical prescriptions and prayers discovered (or invented) by Pope Leo III and given by him to Charles the Great in 800 to protect him against all evils. We extract from it the following:—

Against thieves :—Throw into water the names of the suspected thieves, each written on a piece of paper, and say:—" Aragoni-Parandamo-Eptalicon-Lamboured." At these words one or more of the papers will float; they reveal the names of the guilty.

Against epilepsy :—Blow into the right ear and repeat three times : " Fora consumatio est ramus-malin-rite-confedo-saluero." At these words the patient will give a convulsive start. Drive three nails into the ground at the spot where he fell, and add :—" Valeam de zazoeo attila alleluia."

Against burns :—Place currant jelly on the wound and say three times :—" Escenareth. Fire of God. Lose thy heat-Escenareth ! "

Against toothache :—Say " Struggole faiusque lecutate, te decutinem dolorum persona."

There is a whole book full of these. The above extract will suffice. It will be seen that the Enchiridion is based almost entirely on the power of the word.

Spells

Although we place spells among the Low Magic, later on, in the third part of this book, the scientific explanation of this noted magical practice will be found.

The spell consisted of making in wax a small statue or a heart which was given the name of the enemy to be bewitched. (Sometimes, in order to increase the likeness, this effigy was clothed in the same manner as the hated object, and in order to accentuate the curse it was tried to get a tooth, or hairs, or nail parings of this person, and they were added to the dressing.) After this, concentrating on this image with curses, it was torn with pins, pinched, skinned, crushed. And the enemy endured the same sufferings, even death.

We said that below an explanation of bewitching will be found by reason of the exteriorisation of sensitiveness. But some occultists[1] say that the experiments of Mr. de Rochas in this connection necessitate the magnetisation of the subject who in fact exteriorises his sensitiveness whilst asleep ; but the casters of spells of old never put to sleep those whom they bewitched. And some years ago, when Stanislas de Guaïta and the Abbé Boulan bewitched each other—and both

---

[1] See in this connection R. Schwaeble, *The Book of Luck.*

died of it—they did not put each other to sleep.[1] In the same way (if it is true) the village sorcerers did not put to sleep the cattle and humans on whom they cast their spells and who suffered from them.[2]

It has therefore seemed necessary to find another explanation, an occult one, which is as follows :—There are, if not microbes of passion (good or evil) at any rate *elementals* (see Third Part) who circulate in the Invisible. It is to them that the caster of spells appeals with the whole strength of his faith to induce them to carry to the enemy the poison of illness and of death.

In order to guard against such a curse it is therefore necessary to know a clairvoyant who will warn you of the danger, thanks to which you will, with your own will-power, drive back the accursed messenger who, unable to make use of his " load of evil," throws it back on the sender (this.is called the shock of the rebound).

At bottom there is in the theory of spells an idea similar to that known to Catholic Faith as the " Communion of Saints." We know that Christ " took on Himself the sins of the world " when He died on the cross to save Humanity. We know that various Saints prayed God to put on them the ills of other human beings. An instance is St. Lydwine.[3] We know that people bring to church a limb in wax similar to their ailing limb and ask for it to be healed. We know that Monks pray in the Choir in the hope that their prayers will atone for sins. What is the meaning of all this if not a belief in the possibility of a *transmission of evils* ? Did not Christ heal the possessed by sending the spirits who troubled them into swine ?

.   .   .   .   .   .

Side by side with criminal or hate spells, there are *love spells*.

These are of two kinds—those which stop love and those which evoke it.

The former are called the " tying of the knot " (see below under " Charms.")

We shall deal here with the second alone. We can find as many formulæ for love philtres as we want, either in the old books of spells, or (in the shape of aphrodisiac pills) on the fourth page of the newspapers ! According to Schwaeble, it is at bottom sufficient to rub yourself with verbena. The same writer gives another formula, a mixture consisting of 20 grammes of essence of clove, 10 grammes of essence of geranium and 200 grammes of alcohol at 90 degrees. Wash

---

[1] This extraordinary adventure took place in January, 1893, and was much talked about at the time. Boulan was the first to die, at Lyons, and Guaïta subsequently of the shock of the "rebound."

[2] See in the appendix the enquiry of the *Petit Journal* as to modern witches.

[3] See the admirable book which J. K. Huysmans has written about her ; without being a true occultist, he was very well instructed on these various curious questions of mysticism and demonism.

your hands and arms thoroughly so as to open the pores and then rub yourself with the mixture. It acts, he assures us, on the genetic sense.

What is the meaning of the expression, a charming woman ? It is a woman who *charms*. Whence comes this definite charm of some women ? From their attractions no doubt, but also from some indefinable magical power. Some writers claim that it is because they are able by their will (but without any knowledge of the theory) to influence the good " elementals." Let man do the same, let him exert his will. And by a kind of suggestion he will rouse love in her whom he loves.

Although we are going to speak of spells again later, we have thought it interesting to quote here this extract from an article on the subject by Dr. D. Legué :—

The middle ages with their alternations of shadows and light were never able to fathom magnetism. Antiquity had seen its results without having tried to know their causes. The 18th century, with Mesmer's tub, had not yet disentangled the scientific principle from the miraculous which surrounded it. The same facts which acted on the organism of our fathers are produced to-day.

Not very long ago, Colonel Rochas, a Professor at the Polytechnic School, had gathered round him a few people to whom he intended to demonstrate in an almost tangible form the phenomenon of casting spells in the middle ages. For this purpose he had brought a wax doll, and in support of his theory he thought of one of the ladies in the audience, and said that the person indicated would at the same moment feel his touch of the doll. In fact he touched several times the heart and the arms of the figure, and Mrs. X. felt these touches in a manner proportionate to the will-power which the Professor put into his action.

The experiment over, everybody got up, with the exception of Mrs. X. who was sitting at some distance. One of the spectators out of curiosity picked up the object which the experimenter had used, and turned it over in all directions.

Mrs. X was then heard to say plaintively : "Have you not yet made me suffer enough ? "

How is this singular phenomenon to be explained unless in the same manner as the stigmatisation which reproduces the wounds of the martyrs on the bodies of neurasthenics whose imagination was a prey to trouble caused by religious asceticism ?

Scientists, physicians, physiologists have collected a great number of instances in order to show the pathologic effects produced by violent emotions. Let us go back to an example which has become historic. When persons in convulsions took, on the tomb of the Deacon Paris, the position of Christ on the Cross, it was often noticed that their hands and feet became red. The palms of their hands were burning, and certain marks like stigmata appeared on their bodies. Burdach, the well known physiologist, relates that one day a red spot was seen on the body of a man who had dreamt he had received a violent blow. In this case it is to-day recognised that the intensity of dreams can go so far as to produce the appearance of digestive troubles.

Who has not read, in the *Golden Legend*, the story of the patient of Capriena? Does she not share, with St. Francis of Assisi, Madeleine de Pazzi and so many others, the not very enviable honour of bearing on different parts of her body the stigmata of the Passion? Now " these stigmata, according to Burdin, exude a colourless and burning liquid. It is certain, he adds, that if the bodies of all these bearers of the stigmata had been carefully examined, the same ulcerations and the same pustulas would have been found in them too." Some of them bore piously on their limbs the mysterious traces of the wounds of Christ, their foreheads bled as if under the pressure of the Crown of Thorns. The action of the thought, of the influence of the mind on the body, or, as we should say to-day, auto-suggestion thus became manifest in a material manner.

Well, the followers of occultism ask themselves with some disquietude, could not this volition of the soul act just as well at a distance on a given person? Were there none in the middle ages, who did not wish that their enemy might suffer this or the other torment? Hence the spells which were so frequent in the 13th, 15th and 16th centuries and even later, and which might well be included in the series of phenomena discussed above.

Conjuring Books

These were manuscript books for the use of magicians and sorcerers. They were also called *A.B.C.s of the Devil*. Only three have been printed, and they became famous :—

The *Grimoire of Pope Honorius*.
The *Grimorium Verum*, translated from the Hebrew by Plaigniere.
The *Great Grimoire*, followed by the *Clavicle of Solomon*.

But the following are also looked upon as Conjuring Books :—

The *Enchiridion*, the *Red Dragon*, the *Magical Venus*, the *Treasure of the Old Man of the Pyramids*, the *Magic Works of Agrippa*, the *Secrets of the Old Druid*, the *Black Hen*, etc., and especially *the Great and the Little Albert*.

The last two names are given to the collection of magical formulæ left by Albert the Great, the famous doctor (in the mediæval sense of the word) who was born in Swabia in 1193 and died in Cologne in 1280. Having joined the Order of Dominicans in 1222, he taught the sciences and the philosophy of his day in various towns, and particularly in Paris (1245 to 1248) with such success that in the end he had to speak in the open air, such was the size of his audiences, in a square which has preserved his name (Magister Albertus, which has been corrupted into *Maubert*).

In Rome, in 1255, Pope Alexander IV loaded him with honours, but he soon returned to his beloved studies which he only gave up when overcome by old age. He was the teacher of St. Thomas Aquinas, and his works consist of not less than 20 stout folios. His erudition was amazing. He made real discoveries in chemistry.

But he shared with his times errors which astound us to-day, prodigious childishnesses. He believed in the most grotesque tenets, and it is as a magician that he became historical. He composed hundreds of fantastic receipts which, we repeat, are found in one of his works which has become a classic of its kind, *The admirable Secrets of the Great Albert*, and *The Secrets of the Little Albert*.

Magic Herbs

There are, in Low Magic, about fifteen herbs to which Albert the Great and other sorcerers, ascribe magic virtues, brief details of which we give below :—

The *heliotrope* which, picked in certain conditions, wrapped in a laurel leaf with a wolf's tooth and carried on the person keeps from slander.

The *nettle* which, held in the hand with some yarrow, keeps off the fear of ghosts.

The *teasel* which, dipped into mandragora juice, brings puppies to a bitch.

The *celandine* which, carried on the person together with a mole's heart, makes invincible against enemies and lawsuits.

The *periwinkle* which becomes an aphrodisiac if eaten powdered with earthworms in meat.

The *nept* which, put into the nose of animals, makes them drop as if dead for a short time.

The *hound's-tongue* which, hung round the neck of a dog, gives it a fatal giddiness.

The *henbane* which, mixed with the blood of a young hare and carried on the person, collects round you all the hares of the neighbourhood.

The *lily* which, if picked under the sign of Leo, mixed with the juice of laurel and placed under a dungheap, breeds worms which, powdered and placed in a person's clothes, prevent the latter sleeping.

The *mistletoe* which, hung up to a tree by the wing of a swallow, collects all the cuckoos of the neighbourhood.

The *centaury* which, thrown into the fire on a starry night, makes the stars appear dancing a kind of mad saraband.

The *sage* which, allowed to rot under a dungheap, breeds worms which, thrown into the fire, make a noise like thunder.

The *verbena* which likewise in rich soil breeds worms which, put into a dove-cot, collect pigeons there.

The *mint* which, thrown raw with cypress juice into soup, makes the latter very pleasant to the person eating it.

The *snake-wood*, the *rose*, etc., are also endowed with various marvellous properties.

Side by side with these magical herbs we also have magical animals and stones; each one lends itself to quaint formulæ and fantastic claims which we shall not detail here, for the whole of this section of Magic has to-day fallen into disuse and is without interest.

Let us, however, in passing mention the series of so-called *planetary plants*, which is as follows :—

Offodilius (Saturn). Used against diseases of the kidneys and the legs, and in exorcism.

Buttercup (the Sun).—Against stomach troubles, and to calm frantic and melancholy persons.

Chrinostate (the Moon).—Against acidity and scrofula. Made into tea, it is good for digestion.

Arnoglosse (Mars).—Against headache. Stomachic juice. Cures hæmorrhoids.

Cinquefoil (Mercury).—Closes wounds, calms toothache.

Henbane (Jupiter).—Antidote for ulcers, for liver complaints. Makes cheerful and charming.

Pistorion (Venus).—This is verbena which cleanses the breath and brings love.

Magic Mirrors

They enabled, it was said, to see the present, the past and the future. They are of great variety, and of great antiquity.

St. Augustine (in *De Civitate Dei*, Ch. VII, 35) says that they were used by the witches of Thessaly who wrote their oracles on them in human blood.

Varron claims that they are of Persian origin, the Magi having used them for a method of divination called *Catoptromancy*.

Spartianus says that Didius Julianus used them to know the result of the battle which Tullius Crispinius fought with Septimus Severus, his rival for the Throne.

The persons who, in Rome, read these mirrors were called *Specularii*.

'In the East these instruments were called *Stellar Mirrors*. Pica della Mirandola had faith in them, provided they were made under a favourable constellation, and that they should only be consulted when one felt comfortably warm, for the cold harms the lucidity of their oracle. Reinaud speaks of them in his *Description of the Blacas*

Cabinet. He adds that the operators perfume them, fast for seven days before using them, and recite sacramental prayers at the moment of consulting them. The Chinese and the Hindus made theirs of metal, concave or convex.

Muratori tells us of a Bishop of Verona who was put to death because under his pillow a magic mirror was found bearing on the reverse the word *fiore* which means flower, and proves collaboration with the devil, since, according to St. Cyprian, Satan sometimes appeared in the shape of a flower. A mirror of this kind was also found in the house of Calas de Rienzi. Catherine de Medicis had one.

The shape of these mirrors was, as we have said, very varied. Some bore the name of their inventor (Cagliostro, Swedenborg, etc.) More recently they have been used to fix the eye of clairvoyants or mediums so as to put them into a state of hypnosis.

.　.　.　.　.　.

Cahagnet, in his *Magnetic Magic*, quotes the principal mirrors as follows :—

The Theurgic Mirror—a bottle of clear water looked at by a child, and in which the Archangel Gabriel replies by pictures to his questions·

The Mirror of the Sorcerers—any kind of mirror or pail of water· The country sorcerer, standing near the consultant, recites a spell and shows him the reflection of the picture wanted.

The Mirror of Cagliostro—the bottle of clear water is on a piece of furniture, and before it a child, on whose head the operator places one hand and tells him the questions to ask, to which replies are given in allegorical pictures.

The Mirror of du Potet—a piece of cardboard having pasted on one side a sheet of tin and on the other a piece of black cloth. The operator magnetises it strongly and places it a foot away from the eye of the consultant who, having fixed his eyes on it, soon sees in it the desired object.

The Swedenborgian Mirror—a paste of graphite mixed with olive oil is poured on an ordinary mirror and allowed to dry for a few days. The consultant, whose image must not be reflected (he stands at some distance for this reason) looks into it, whilst the operator stares magnetically at the back of his head, and vision takes place.

The Magnetic Mirror—a round crystal globe filled with magnetised water at which the consultant looks carefully until the desired vision appears.

The Narcotic Mirror—similar globe but a narcotic powder made of belladonna, henbane, mandragora, hemp, poppy, etc., is dissolved in the water.

The Galvanic Mirror—it is made of two discs, one of copper and concave, the other of zinc and convex, both magnetised nine times in nine days. The centre of the concave is looked at.

Cabalistic Mirrors—there are seven, being seven globes each representing one of the seven planets of Astrology, made of the corresponding metal and consulted on the appropriate astrological day. They are :—

The globe of the Sun, made of gold and consulted on Sundays as to superior beings and the great persons of the earth.

The globe of Mercury, made of a glass globe filled with mercury and consulted on Wednesdays as to questions of money.

The globe of Jupiter, made of tin and consulted on Thursdays as to the probability of success and as to the devotion of domestics.

The globe of Mars, made of iron and consulted on Tuesdays as to quarrels, lawsuits, enmities.

The globe of Venus, made of copper and consulted on Fridays as to questions of love.

The globe of Saturn, made of lead and consulted on Saturdays as to secrets, lost articles, etc.

The globe of the Moon, made of silver and consulted on Mondays as to dreams and plans.

As regards Mirrors, the Third Part will give information as to everything relating to " crystal vision," a phenomenon of clairvoyance pure and simple, and there will be shown the psychic basis of these apparently fantastic magic objects where it is no longer necessary to evoke the spirits and where it is possible *actually* to obtain visions of the future.

Divination by coffee grounds, as we have said, is nothing but a substitute for divination by magic mirrors.

Mandragora

This curious plant has a root which somewhat resembles a human face or a phallus. [1] Some mystics saw in it the umbilical sign of our terrestrial origin. Eliphas Lévi himself thought that man having been made of the dust of the earth, must needs have first been made in the shape of a root. By analogy he inferred that the first men belonged to the family of mandragoras, some of the latter having come to life under the sun. It is difficult for a naturalist to admit this hypothesis. However it may be, some alchemists believed in it. Paracelsus claimed that it was possible to succeed in everything with the aid of mandragora, and also by its means to give birth to a homunculus (little living man).

[1] We deal here with *Atropa mandragora*, the apothecary's kind, also called female mandragora, hand of glory or magician's herb, with a foetid smell, and often a forked root.

Hence also artificial mandragora was made and was used as a talisman.

Necromancy

This was the art of raising the dead. The celebrated Christian, in his *History of Magic* which the astrologer Ely Star used so much, taught this art, of which much might be said if one takes into account the phenomena of spiritualism or even of mediumship (see Third Part). There is certainly some connection between modern experiments and the old practices of witchcraft, for it is more than probable that more than one sorcerer was a medium.

The celebrated Voisin, that remarkable witch, soothsayer and poisoner, burned alive in 1680, practised necromancy. And in the *Black Magic* of the doctors Jaf and Caufeynon we find the account of the evocation of the ghost of Turenne carried out by her in the Church of Saint Denis at the request of Abbé d'Auvergne, Prince and Cardinal de Bouillon, the heir of the Marshal who believed that the latter had hidden a treasure.

The description of an evocation ceremony is found in the same book, and in many others to which we refer the reader, begging him however to beware of this kind of witchcraft which could only end in turning his brain. It will be better to confine himself to the experiments of mediumistic apparitions which he will find farther on.

Many have erroneously included in the same word both Goetia or Black Magic and Necromancy. But the latter raises the dead, and Goetia raises demons. According to the Count de Resie, this raising of the spirits of ancestors was merely performed in the way of family affection. The Canaanites practised it. Moses forbade it to the Jews as being opposed to the worship of the true God.

It will be remembered that the Witch of Endor raised Samuel for Saul. Other necromancers are Orpheus, Phorontius, Cecrops, Apollonius of Thyana, Jamblichus, Porphyrius. Shakespeare used this magic art with powerful effect in his theatre (the three Witches in Macbeth put into their cauldron all the ingredients mentioned in the traditional formulæ).

Pacts

These were agreements, treaties entered into with the Devil with the view to obtaining special favours from him. They took the form of direct and formal agreements, or invocations through the intermediary of sorcerers, or acts which were to take effect through the power of the Prince of Darkness.

The method of entering into these agreements is found mainly in the *Great Clavicle of Solomon,* which contains the *Pacta conventa dæmoniorum.* First we learn the names of the infernal dignitaries— Lucifer, the Emperor of Hell, Prince Beelzebub, the Grand Duke Astaroth; the military chiefs Lucifuge, Satanachia, Fleurty, etc., the subordinates Baal, Agares, etc. After this the procedure, the method of invocation, etc., are stated.

These invocations vary according to what is asked for, such as increasing one's property, finding a treasure, winning the loved woman, etc.

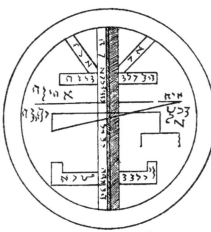

THE GREAT PENTACLE OF SOLOMON.

The ink for the pacts was made of river water, gall-nut, Roman vitriol, alum, gum arabic, the whole heated in a new vessel over a fire of vines cut during the full moon of March and ferns cut at midnight on St. John's Eve.

Pentacles

There are two kinds of pentacles, some universal (for invocations and spells), the others personal.

Pentacles, says Pierre Piobb, are not talismans. The latter assist in the polarisation of fluids, whereas pentacles contain the polarised fluids. Talismans are intermediaries, pentacles generators.

In making them the following are required :—

1. Draw a sacred symbol and enclose it in a double circle.
2. Inscribe within this double circle a sacred name or an appropriate verse from the sacred books.
3. Perfume it with the perfume of the planet the nature of which corresponds to the purpose.
4. Sing Psalms, cast spells, make incantations, if necessary offer sacrifices.

The pentacle is drawn on a Wednesday at the hour of Mercury when the Moon is in a sign of air or earth and in the same degree as the sun.

A pentacle must be engraved on metal corresponding to the planet whence it comes, or else on virgin parchment or china.

LOW MAGIC

Magic Perfumes

We mention a few as curiosities :—

Friday's Perfume :—Musk, ambergris, aloe wood, red roses, the whole reduced to powder, mixed with the blood of doves and the brain of sparrows, made into a paste, then into grains, and consecrated with the following words :—" Deus Abraham, Deus Isaac, Deus Jacob, bless all the creatures of the kinds contained in these odorous grains, so that they may increase the power and the virtue of their scent, that no enemy or phantom may abide in them. Per Dominum nostrum. Amen."

Monday's Perfume :—The day of the Moon, frog's head, bull's eyes, seed of white poppy, pure incense such as storax or benzoin with a little camphor. The whole mixed with the blood of a turtledove, made into a paste, then into grains. And with it the magical operations of Monday are performed.

Quaint formulæ certainly. The Church is opposed to these contrivances. And yet do we not see in the pages of Holy Writ, in the story of Tobit, the angel leading him and commanding him, when he meets his wife, not to fail to make a perfume with the liver of a fish whom the angel had cut open, so that through the *occult power of that perfume* evil spirits might be restrained from harming him and be kept away from the bridal couch ?

And after all what is the incense of religious rites but a survival of the magic of perfumes ?

Philters and Charms

Philters are mystic drinks producing certain sentiments ; those relating to love are the most sought after. There were also some for inspiring hate, courage, etc. Here is a specimen :—Dried periwinkle powdered and mixed with powdered earthworm induces love. A pinch dropped into food is sufficient to excite him who swallows it. As will be seen, philters and aphrodisiacs are not unrelated.

So-called sacred plants usually entered into the composition of philters, such as thyme, marjoram, fennel, wild mint, hyssop, lily. Also some ashes like those of the dried heart of a dove, of a donkey's hoof, etc.

Lustral water was a powerful philter. It used to be obtained as follows :—In a fountain of white marble the magicians collected storm water and at the end of five years killed in this thirteen doves, a virgin trout, a sheep, a bull, a black cat and a white dog. Then it was put into crystal flagons, and subsequently used for aspersions accompanied by incantations. The Holy Water of to-day is simpler. But he who uses it must not laugh at lustral water. Instead of lustral water a philter may be made of rain water in which for thirteen days thirteen kinds of sacred plants and the powder of a dove's heart are soaked.

The sap of the hazelnut tree, the water from chick peas and hellebore seeds mixed, the water of garlic and pomegranates are also good philters.

Charms are spells in the shape of words arranged in a certain way which are used to obtain miraculous effects. But there are also charms without words. Thus La Voisin claims to have received from a priest consecrated oils which made lips loving, and she promised some to Madame de Baucé.

Enchantment was a kind of charm by means of song or music. Some snake charmers charm by movements of the eye. Others charm by playing the flute. The delightful legend of Orpheus will be remembered.

Domestic, Culinary, Medical and other Prescriptions

Cloth is made non-inflammable by washing it in salted water after having rubbed it with alum beaten up in the white of an egg.

To be able to handle red hot iron, rub your hands with red arsenic and alum mixed in the juice of leek and laurel gum.

Scorpions and snakes are driven out of a house by burning the lung of a donkey in it.

To prevent rats from coming into your house, burn the hoof of a horse.

To catch birds, scatter grain which has been soaked in wine lees and the juice of hemlock. Those which eat them will not be able to fly away.

The seed of leek restores its strength to vinegar which has gone off.

Crush and mix together marigold blooms, marjoram, wheaten flour, stale butter, goat's grease and earthworms, and you will obtain excellent bait for fishes.

To get rid of fleas, sprinkle the room with water in which zinc sulphate has been dissolved.

For sunburn, rub yourself at night with an ointment made of oil of sweet almonds, wax and camphor.

To prevent apples rotting, rub them with mint juice.

The size of eggs is increased by mixing diluted red chalk in the hens' food.

Chewing sorrel leaves is a good aperient.

To cure a drunkard, make him drink wine in which an eel has been drowned.

For sciatica use cow dung cooked under cinders in vine or cabbage leaves.

Hot cow dung also cures the sting of bees, hornets, wasps, etc.

Gallienus cured tumours and callouses on the knee with a paste made of goat dung diluted in barley flour and oxycrate.

For boils and carbuncles, sheep dung diluted in vinegar and made into a poultice.

For burns, fowl dung diluted in oil of roses.

Raw corn well chewed and put on a tumour brings it to a head.

Cooked in goose fat, earthworms cure earache. Drunk in wine they dissolve calculus. Swallowed in honey and water they cure jaundice.

The ash of elm, oak, maple, ivy, birch, is an astringent. Gallienus also used it to stop nose bleeding.

Rotten wood, placed on a purulent ulcer, cleanses and closes it.

Cobweb put on a cut stops bleeding.

To relieve a fit of the gout, apply the skinned root of henbane. The juice of the same plant, mixed with honey, eases liver troubles.

The root of verbena, made into a poultice, cures fistulas, ulcers, hæmorrhoids.

The ash of frogs makes an excellent depilatory.

Goat's horn, reduced to ash, strengthens the gums and stops dysentery.

Boiled snails quickly reduce œdema.

Hare's brain is a good emollient which facilitates the coming of the first teeth.

Fine chimney soot mixed with good vinegar is a specific against chilblains.

To avoid getting drunk, take before your meal a spoonful of olive oil mixed, if possible, with two spoonfuls of betony water.

An infusion of parsley is good for women if their periods are irregular.

We stop here, and advise a physician rather than any of these medical formulas, a good cook rather than the culinary ones. But at the same time an interesting book might be written by studying, commenting and dealing critically with the thousands of ancient prescriptions, many of which must be left alone, but a great number of which, particularly those which include simples and herbs, might be tested in the light of modern experience and knowledge.

Satanism

In his preface to *Satanism and Magic* by Jules Bois, J. K. Huysmans divides the " Realm of the Fallen Angel " into two camps, Palladists and Luciferians. We leave High Freemasonry to deal with the Palladists, and will briefly speak of the Luciferians who have an Antipope, the head of a kind of parody of the Vatican. At the time of Huysmans, this black Holy Father, installed in the infernal Rome at Charleston, was a man of the name of Lemmi. His disciples follow a kind of reverse Catholicism and worship " the God of Evil," whilst the Palladists see in Satan the true Adonai, the Element of Goodness. In both cases, it will be seen, there is faith in the Devil.[1]

A very old faith indeed. Luciferism is nothing but an off-shoot of Manichæism. Its attraction lies in the fact that it includes apostate priests, thieves of the Host, supporters of sacrilege, such as the Canon Docre created by the author of *Là-Bas*.

Formerly, as we have seen, Satanism invaded Witchcraft (Sabbath, raising of Evil Spirits, etc.) Various books, among them one by Jules Bois, contain complete descriptions of scenes of black magic, the Sabbath itself, diabolic confessions and pacts, ancient black masses. But it is well known that the cult of Satan has not died out, and that even in our days modernised black masses have been and are being said. Some of them, called " Offices of the vain Observance," perpetuate the Albigense heresy. Others, in the 17th century, were called " sacrilegious masses of Guibourg," and had the added horror of the killing of a child on the wanton nakedness of a woman. Then there is the extraordinary Mass according to Ezechiel and according to Vintras described by Huysmans, who also speaks of one which he claims to be used in the dark and distant district of Vaugirard. We are assured that all these black follies are by no means fallen into disuse yet.[2]

Other devilries were incubi and succubi, connections between women and devils, devils and mystics. These queer connections abounded in olden times, at least in imagination, and even in the 19th century we see a man like Caudenberg tell of his relations with the Virgin (about 1854), and a whole series of demoniac connections arises in brains which are overexcited by eroticism, and tales of vampirism. We have no wish to go into these follies, and only mention them to show the survival of Witchcraft, and the danger which lies in not confining Occultism to the great and splendid data which are sufficient to make it interesting and magnificent.

Sorcery and Curses

Here are some curses which it is possible to put on others or to receive, together with the means of escaping them, if we are to believe a little book by Professor Asmodeus :—

[1] See, in the Appendix, the enquiry of Messrs. Nadaud and Pelletier, into modern witches and satanists.

[2] Here, as in the Sabbath, a kind of erotic sadism induces practices which seem most blasphemous. And almost always the Black Mass uses a naked woman as altar on which the Host is defiled.

Knots.—" Tying the knot." This is used against lovers or newly married couples. Go to the place where the lovers or the newly married couple usually meet. As soon as you see them, quickly tie a knot in a lace which you have in your hand. Watch their eyes, and as soon as they look at each other, make a second knot. The knot is tied, especially if the appropriate magical words have been uttered. The couple is bewitched, and their love is accursed.

To turn this curse aside, you must turn your wedding ring three times round the finger, and wear on your breast the sacred guardian stone of destinies.

Spider.—To turn aside the bad luck due to seeing a spider in the morning or at noon, pick up some dust and throw it on to the spot where the spider passed, saying " Ada." " Ada " is a well known magic word.

The Evil Eye. Curse is another word for this. The chief curses are the evil eye or jettatura, and the casting of spells. As to the casting of spells, see under that heading. As to the evil eye, most Italians firmly believe in it, and to turn it aside use a little horn of coral and turn it point forward towards any one who " casts the evil eye," muttering the word " corna."

Obsessions.—To cure them, says the *Book of Black Science,* cook a calf's foot, make it into a paste with goose fat, cinnamon and pepper, and rub it on your chest seven days in succession.

Vampirism

In Magic this is the act of one human being sucking up the vital fluid of another human being. The Vampire acts for himself or for a third party. As will be seen, it is to some extent the opposite of magnetism.

Fluid vampirism, says Pierre Piobb, takes many forms. As soon as one person dominates another, he consciously or not withdraws vital fluid from him. Some people use their friends for the purpose of increasing their own nervous energy. This happens in the case of " arrivists," people without heart who drop their connections as soon as they have ceased to be useful.

" Faith " is a phenomenon of magic vampirism in this sense that the operator uses vampirism to form a strong single-minded *eggregore* (group consciousness). This is for instance what Christ did with his apostles.

The " evil eye " is also a kind of vampirism ; as we have seen it is turned aside by a movement of the hand in shape of a horn.

Any one fearing some evil from a chance meeting may disperse the dangerous fluid of the person met by touching iron, this metal being a good conductor which carries the fluid down to the earth, provided it touches the ground.

III

Good Luck and Bad Luck

We shall not here take the part of either " strong minds " or " weak minds." We shall confine ourselves to saying that very many " strong minds " have secret dreads and sometimes unconfessed superstitions, and that among the " weak minds " are to be found numbers of scientists, men of genius and military and other celebrities.

We find in this 20th century of ours some airman who takes a black cat up with him as his mascot, a boxer making the sign of the cross before entering the ring, an actress who never goes on the stage without having made a cross of two matches, or a courtesan burning a candle to obtain success in love.

Let us all search into the very bottom of our hearts and ask ourselves if we have not at some time or other, in certain circumstances, sought some thing which brings luck or avoided some other which may bring ill luck. We all more or less believe in good luck and in bad luck of which we will now say a few words.

Lucky and Unlucky Presents

For the sake of information only let us draw up first tables of those articles which, according to Tradition, carry good or bad luck, offering our apologies for any repetition there may be of information given previously under other headings.

TABLE OF PRESENTS GIVEN BY A MAN TO A WOMAN

Bringing good luck	Bringing bad luck
1. JEWELS	1. JEWELS
Rings of gold or silver without stones or pearls, or with a black pearl, ruby, sapphire, diamond, cameo.	Rings of glass or cut stone.
Gold or silver chain bracelet.	Ring of gold or silver with fine pearls or turquoise, amethyst, aquamarine, opal, coral, jet.
Jewelled buttons.	Locket (risk of quarrel or break).
Ear-rings in rings, diamonds, pearls, emeralds.	Pin (tie, hair or hat) unless it is set with a lucky stone and has been exchanged for a penny with a hole in it.
Brooch (if a penny with a hole in it is given in exchange).	
Watch (with inscription engraved).	
Necklace with odd number of pearls.	

LOW MAGIC

Bringing good luck

2. VARIOUS ARTICLES

A magnet.
An album.
A jewel case.
A shawl.
A crystal cup.
An *engraved* gold or silver thimble
A tooth set as a jewel.
A stole (fur or silk).
A pair of gloves.
A book.
A lamp.
An engraved medal.
A Chinese vase.
Vases.
A spinning wheel with its spindle full.
A picture.
A violin.

3. FLOWERS

Rose (white or red).
White and red carnation.
Lily, convolvulus, clematis, mistletoe.
Daisy, lilac, clover, wall-flower.
Hawthorn, everlasting flower, cornflower.
Poppy, forget-me-not.
Four-leaved clover.

4. FRUITS

Grapes (white or black).
Pomegranates, oranges.
A divided almond of which he keeps the other half.

5. SCENTS

Carnation, rose, violet.
Wallflower, amber, fern.
Cut hay, and generally all sweet scents.

Bringing bad luck

2. VARIOUS ARTICLES

A wooden box.
A handkerchief.
A portrait.
A nail file.
A belt.
A scarf.
A pair of shoes.
An umbrella.
A looking-glass.
Curtains.
A nail.
A trunk.
A hair.
Cotton.
Tongs.
A note book, a pencil.
An ink pot, a pen.
A knife.

3. FLOWERS

Briar, bramble, cypress, holly.
Hemlock, nettle, tuberose, cyclamen.
Poppy, jonquil, autumn colchicum.
Digitalis, moss, grass.
And generally all green and all poisonous plants.

4. FRUITS

Chestnuts.
Wild plum.
Dried figs.
Pears.

5. SCENTS

Trefle incarnat, bergamot.
Musk, patchouli, ylang-ylang.
And generally all strong perfumes.

TABLE OF PRESENTS GIVEN BY A WOMAN TO A MAN

Bringing good luck	Bringing bad luck
1. JEWELS	**1. JEWELS**
A plain *engraved* ring of gold or silver or set with a coloured stone.	A card-case.
A watch with inscription engraved.	A sovereign-case.
A chain (first thrown into the water).	A locket.
A pearl tie pin.	Cuff links.
	Studs.
	A cigar-case.
	A cigarette-case.
2. VARIOUS ARTICLES	
A walking stick (mahogany, oak or malacca).	**2. VARIOUS ARTICLES**
Gloves.	A purse.
Tobacco.	A portrait.
A cup.	A tie or a hat.
A writing table.	A key, a pin or a nail.
A picture.	An inkpot or a strong box.
	Linen (a handkerchief, etc.)
3. FLOWERS	**3. FLOWERS**
Red or white rose.	Peony, geranium.
Camellia and gardenia.	Glycinia, acacia.
Violet and cornflower.	Periwinkle, columbine.
And specially pansy.	And all yellow flowers.
4. FRUITS	**4. FRUITS**
Apples, plums, peaches.	Medlar.
Mandarines and grapes.	Nut.
5. SCENTS	**5. SCENTS**
Lavender (sweetness).	Generally
Iris (tender promise).	All strong scents.

Lucky and Unlucky Days

Generally considered lucky are :—

Monday, the day of the Moon : calm and sweetness.
Wednesday, the day of Mercury : success.
Thursday, the day of Jupiter : courage and will-power.
Sunday, the day of the Lord : joy and repose.

On the other hand considered unlucky are :—

Tuesday, the day of Mars : struggles, quarrels, failure.
Friday, the day of Venus : passion (in Rome the Senate did not sit on Friday)
Saturday, the day of Saturn : danger, death.

LOW MAGIC

A Hindu belief, dating back to Sanscrit times, credited the hours also with good or bad influence. The unfavourable hour (Irâghon Kâlam, commonly called Rakalon) is balanced by the hour of good omen (Khonlighei Kâlam). The following table has been compiled for the hours of each day of the week, the hours being numbered from one to twenty-four for the sake of convenience.

Days	Lucky Hours	Unlucky Hours
Sunday	.. From 15 to 16.30 o'clock.	.. From 16.30 to 18 o'clock.
Monday	.. From 13.30 to 15 o'clock	.. From 7.30 to 9 o'clock.
Tuesday	.. From 12 to 13.30 o'clock	.. From 15 to 16.30 o'clock
Wednesday	.. From 10 to 12 o'clock	.. From 12 to 13.30 o'clock
Thursday	.. From 9 to 10.30 o'clock	.. From 13.30 to 15 o'clock
Friday	.. From 7.30 to 9 o'clock	.. From 10.30 to 12 o'clock
Saturday	.. From 6 to 7.30 o'clock	.. From 9 to 10.30 o'clock

Cledomancy

Cledomancy was the name of the science of words bringing good or bad luck, fatidic or conjuring words.

Here is a table of them, but it is unnecessary to say that we only give it by way of information, to show how far some people went in their faith in the magic power of the word.

Fatidic Words

Abbe.	Steel.	Needle.	Atheist.
Cabala.	Sorrow.	Chaos.	Heaven.
Devil.	Bury.	By the Blue Blood.	By my Mother.
Credo.	Alas !	Horns of the Devil.	By Satan !
Miracle !	Motus.	Vlan !	Werewolf.
Good God !	By God !	Death.	Ghost.
Phantom.			

Conjuring Words

Ada.[1]	Per ada.[2]	Ada rama.	I ada.
Soloma.	Perdidi.	Dulco.	Felix.
Deo.	Gratias.	Ignoto .	Bene.
Ada lux.	Lux.	Exegi.	Festina.
Simpre.	Finis.	Hie.	Ada.
Ada.	Ada.	Anima.	Fortunate.
Corpus.			

[1] The mere uttering of the magic word "ada" preserves from bad luck. Good luck is sure if you say it every morning and every evening, turning towards the North and the South.

[2] The combination of the two Magic words "ada et sacramente" has special virtues, all of good omen.

WORDS BRINGING GOOD LUCK

Good.	Well.	Perfect.	Sun.
Isis.	Io.	Eol.	Luck.
Dia.			

WORDS BRINGING BAD LUCK

Hell.	Curse.	Bad luck. [1]	Ill luck.
Pitch.	Sticky.	Damned.	Misery.
Misfortune.			

Etymological Analogies

Whereas the word *chance* comes from an expression in the game of dice, the word *chéance* (the act of falling) denotes the number of pips shown by the fallen dice. Chance became *veine* (good luck) at the time of the rush of the goldseekers to California, the *vein* being strictly speaking different in its composition from the rock of which it formed part. Then, as the *filon* is a kind of thread of precious metal running through the rock, like a vein in the human body, but which it sometimes takes many long days to find, this word also became a popular synonym for luck. From *veine* by analogy came the word *déveine*, its opposite. If the *déveine* (bad luck)persists, it becomes *guigne* or *guignon*, in slang the *sticker* or *pitch*. The mere saying of the last two words brings bad luck.

And yet good and bad luck are the result not so much of chance as of qualities and defects. Good luck is generally worked up to by will-power, prudence, foresight (sometimes instinctive, unconscious), bad luck results from a series of carelessness, lack of energy, unsustained effort. It will be well, therefore, to count first of all on ourselves so that good luck may subsequently help us and bad luck leave us.

Nonetheless good luck and bad luck do exist. But it has been noticed that good luck not brought about or sustained by effort does not last, and that sudden fortunes are usually unstable.

One evening when Taglioni had had a very great success on the stage, a young dancer came up and said to her :

"Ah, you have good luck."

"True," said the star, "but I cultivate it every day."

"You have perhaps a talisman," said the girl, who did not understand.

"Come and see me to-morrow at home, and I will show it to you."

The dancer went to see Taglioni and was present at a long series of exercises, at the end of which the famous artist sank exhausted into an armchair and said :

[1] Use as synonyms " the thing " or " the cherry," and if by chance you say the fatal word, quickly touch wood to avert the evil fate

LOW MAGIC

" You see my talisman, it is called *work*."
An apt lesson. But it does not alter the fact that good and bad luck do exist.

Fetishes

The belief in fetishes involves the belief in obscure powers which dwell hidden in certain objects, which generally by their shape evoke the idea of incantation. Such for instance are the coral horns so highly valued in Italy, because they recall those of the devil, and that wearing them will prevent Satan, flattered by this imitation, to cause us worries. So also it is certain that the superstition which credits some animals with the power of bringing good or bad luck, and which is accounted for by some striking detail (the owl, son of the Night, with its silent flight, for instance, the bat dwelling in ruins, the swallow messenger of spring, etc.), is the result of many coincidences carefully collected.

But it must also be noted—and this is a matter of psychology— that the fetish often has a real power, due to the esteem in which it is held and the fact that it *puts you into a state of self-confidence thanks to which success is more likely*. It was due to the knowledge of this truth that Mahommed obtained miracles of bravery from his troops in his battles by assuring them that thousands of angels fought by their side; sustained by this illusion they fought with redoubled ardour and often were victorious.

In short the fetish is *an assurance against weakness*. What, then, matters the origin of its power, if it brings triumph?

On the other hand one observation has been made at all times, it is that Luck comes to a man at least once in his life, sometimes twice and thrice. Woe to him then who does not see it or does not know how to grasp it.

But the belief in Good Luck is not without its danger; it entails the belief in Bad Luck, in which no one ought ever to believe, for it stops all initiative through fear of failure. Luck does not favour hesitation. *Audaces fortuna juvat!* Good luck goes to the daring. Daring is the source of almost all success, and only the timid will believe in his bad luck.

Further Notes on Good Luck

To say of some one, " He has had luck " means that Good Luck visited him at a specified moment. To say, " He is lucky " means that it is with him constantly.

Now what is Good Luck if not a chain of fortunate events, each· one of which has its cause? Is the chance which thus connects them the result of an occult will? Is it the mere unforeseen meeting of the elements which constitute the former? In any case it has a cause like every phenomenon, but this cause is more or less easy to discover. And it is because there is one or more causes that a directing will may and can succeed in invoking a power which is greater. This is why Good Fortune nearly always responds to the persistent appeal of sustained effort.

We must assist luck. It is not by remaining inactive, by despising letters, efforts, connections, etc., that we succeed in any matter, of whatsoever kind it may be. Nor is it by remaining ignorant of ourselves, our abilities, tendencies, characteristics, etc. In order to be *lucky*, begin by thoroughly knowing yourself, by discovering your instincts, your tastes, your qualities, and also your defects. Then give to your " personal chances " the frame, the surroundings which suit them, the food necessary to their development. Theoretically, observes R. Schwaeble,[1] a man who knows himself thoroughly, by means of the occult sciences, would be able to use all his qualities and restrain all his defects, and would succeed in everything. And it is the fact.

. . . . . .

Luck is often only the ability to grasp the opportunities offered by chance. But this ability comes of an aptitude which itself comes from qualities of observation, patience, daring. The example of great men who have been called *lucky* proves that if Chance did call upon them, they in fact knew how to recognise it and turn it to account.

No doubt Napoleon would not have had the opportunity of proving his exceptional qualities of organiser and military chief in less troublous times, but it was through his genius that he made use of this coincidence. No doubt Jenner, when a student, was lucky to hear a feverish peasant, suspected of smallpox, say that she could not possibly have it, as " she had already had the *Cow's disease*," this expression giving rise to the idea of vaccine ; but had this chance not been offered to other doctors, who had neglected to make use of it ?

. . . . . .

Papus, in a chapter of his remarkable *Book of Luck* called " The Woman of the World," but which may be applied to everyone, men and women, draws a very apt comparison between luck, or rather bad luck, and slander.

Here, he says, we have a woman of the world, intelligent, beautiful and wealthy, whose good fortune seems to be lasting. But, one day, suddenly the golden dream flies away, bad luck settles down at her hearth, troubles, catastrophes succeed each other. Who is mysteriously responsible for this upheaval? The woman herself, who spent her time at home speaking and allowing to be spoken evil of others.

[1] *The Book of Luck.*

Thus Evil sowed its seeds, dug its roots, grew its stem—and its fruits.

People smiled at these slanders in the drawing room of the lady; she was thought smart; unkind remarks about one or the other, sometimes her best friends, were amusing. But the friends and others ended by knowing that evil was being spoken of them. Squabbles arose, relations were broken off; and this was the beginning of the ills which soon poured down upon the House of Slander. Friends, relatives, no longer gave good advice, good " tipsters " no longer tried to be useful to the lovely chatterbox or to her husband, no longer gave warning of this or that risk, being in their turn glad to harm those who harmed others. Bad investments followed, good business disappeared, assistance of all kinds was lacking. And as everything stands together, in Society as in the Universe, the isolated House in the end collapsed.

Moral :—Never speak evil of others. Never allow it to be spoken in front of you. Protect absent friends. Contradict evil reports. And it will be said of you that you are good, faithful and sure. And you will be loved. Being loved, you will be assisted in those thousand different ways which favour, or rather which create, good luck.

IV

The Language of Flowers

Everybody loves flowers. The rich man has expensive ones in his beds and his hothouses; the poor man, the working girl, the little sempstress have modest ones which smile in their window boxes. Poets have sung the charm of flowers which are the symbol of a life all too short but sometimes so perfumed by joy, tenderness or art. None is insensible to the beauty of their petals, even those who in other matters are cold or dry at heart.

Whence comes this fascination ? Perhaps it is because there are no ugly flowers. Amongst animals there are toads, spiders, black-beetles, repulsive beasts. But does any flower cause dislike ? Each one is sympathetic by its beauty, or its scent, or its daintiness.

And then the flower is sun and cheerfulness. Flowers perfume the days of spring, embellish summer, make autumn bearable, sometimes even defy winter. They bring eternal charm to Nature and into the Home.

" The flower," writes Chateaubriand divinely, " is the daughter of Morning, the charm of spring, the source of perfume, the fascination of the virgin, the love of the poet. It fades quickly like man, but it gently returns its leaves to earth. The essence of its perfumes is preserved—they are thoughts which survive it. In days of old it crowned the cup at the banquet and the white hair of the wise man. The early Christians used it to cover their martyrs and the altar in the catacombs. To-day and in memory of those olden times we place it in our temples. We attribute our affections to its colours, hope to its leaves, innocence to its whiteness, chastity to its delicate tints."

Flowers are loved. They are made into nōsegays for pretty women, the beloved betrothed, the gentle wife. They decorate our furniture, our balconies, our altars. Their petals are slipped into our love letters, they are dried in our books. At festivals they are offered to our parents, our friends, our chiefs. They are brought to weddings. They are placed on the tomb. They are brought into sacred and profane matters. They are seen at the ball and in Church.

There are flowers everywhere—in the valley, in the woods and the fields, at the water's edge, on the slope of mountains. There is no plain which has not its own kind, and the beautiful blue thistle blooms even in the driest of sand dunes.

Flowers accompany us in our happiness and in our sorrow. They comfort the patient by brightening his dull room. With their sweetness they intoxicate the boudoir of the loved woman and the den of the bachelor. They are the friends of all our days. They speak.

Yes, they have been given a language. Legend credits this stratagem of lovers communicating by the voice of flowers to the adventure of a young Arab who loved a Pasha's daughter. It was Axiania who invented this means of chattering with Mohammed without saying anything simply through the flowers which she tended. Through her was born the Selam or language of flowers.

The following selams or speaking nosegays are quoted by some old writers :—

Thuya + Clover + periwinkle + pink carnation = My heart will not alter.—May I hope ?—My friendship will last for life.—My faithfulness is equal to all tests.

Another :—Thyme + rosemary + elder + white jasmine + convolvulus + mignonette + everlasting flower = The sight of you thrills me. Your presence scatters my trouble. You comfort me in every sorrow. You are amiable and charm me. Your qualities surpass your charms. Always yours. My friendship is without end.

Yet another :—Forget-me-not, pansies, white carnation and veronica together say :—Do not forget me, for I think of you ; my love is great and pure and I give you my heart.

And yet another :—Absinthe with hydrangea, balsam and helenia —The pain which your indifference and your disdain cause me is the reason for my tears.

LOW MAGIC

A well arranged nosegay takes the place of a letter, lacks its perils, and for the timid, its disadvantages. A nosegay is never indiscreet, compromising or disrespectful, whilst at the same time occasionally it is not without daring.

. . . . . .

In the following table will be found the thoughts suggested by flowers or the words whose place they take. They are not always the same with all writers. Some legendary and easily explained meanings are found everywhere. Thus for instance the honeysuckle and the ivy are signs of attachment ; the stinging thistle a sign of revenge ; the everlasting flower a sign of faithfulness, etc. It is with this aim in view that we have modified various meanings so as to bring them more into accord with the symbol of the plant. Occasionally we have preserved two or three well known meanings.

But in all these cases we should strongly advise lovers who wish to avail themselves of these mute dialogues, each to buy this book and to cross out in pencil every double or triple meaning so as to leave only one clear one for each flower. Neglect of this precaution might cause misunderstandings and even calamities !

. . . . . .

The following are the traditional meanings given to a certain number of flowers :—

A

Absinthe—Heartache, absence, separation.
Apricot (flower · of)—Timid love.
Acacia—Platonic love. Also, you are all grace and elegance.
Acanthus—Love of art. Also, nothing will be able to separate us.
Achilleia—Disputes, quarrels.
Aconite—Your disdain will kill me.
Amaranth—Constancy (its name means, which does not fade).
Amaryllis—Pride, vanity. You are too fond of shining.
Anemone—Break. Go away ! (reminder of the flighty nymph Anemone).
Angelica—Inspiration. I am in ecstasy (Angel).
Aristolochus—You are a tyrant ! (Powerful juice and large leaves).
Asphodel—I regret the past.
Aster—Daintiness. Also, have you really told me the truth ?
Azalea—Your passion is fragile and ephemeral. Barren regrets. (Fatal gift).

B

Balsam—You have offended me. You are cold.
Basil—I hate you. Also, I am poor (Basil was an emblem of poverty).
Begonia—Beware ! I am fanciful.
Belladonna—I bring bad luck (fatal gift).
Buttercup—Mockery, don't laugh at me. Also spite.

Blackthorn—How many obstacles there are to our love !
Box (always green)—I never change. Stoicism in adversity.
Briar—I love solitude.
Bilberry—Confession of deceit.
Bugloss—Lies. You are falseness personified.
Bramble—Envy. Jealousy. Injustice.
Barberry—You are a bad lot.
Burdock—You bore me.
Burnet—You are my only love.
Bindweed—Passing friendship without results.

C

Camellia—Constancy. I shall love you always.
Camomile—I am always devoted to you.
Campanula (Mirror of Venus)—You are charming but somewhat proud.
Centaury—Our love is perfect happiness.
Colchicum—Our pleasant time is over. Let us separate (this is an autumn
flower).
Columbine—I am madly in love with you (its bell shaped flower resembles
a fool's staff).
Convolvulus—You are a coquette. Also, humble perseverance.
Cornflower—Daintiness. Innocent charm. Heavenly heart.
Cinquefoil—Walk by moonlight. Also, I love my family.
Cedar (red)—My parents are dissatisfied.
Carnation (white)—You inspire me with pure sentiments.
Carnation (red)—You inspire me with worldly sentiments.
Carnation (pink)—I answer you favourably.
Carnation (purple)—You inspire me with antipathy.
Carnation (double)—I must think.
Carnation (Sweet William)—You are perfect.
Clover—Doubt, uncertainty. May I hope ?
Clover (yellow)—I should like to, at once.
Clover (red)—You do please me !
Clover (purple)—I am staying at home.
Cyclamen—Good-bye.
Cypress (the tree of the grave)—Our love is dead. Regrets and tears.

D

Daffodil—You are deceiving me.
Dahlia—Barren abundance (it has no scent). Many words but no soul.
Digitalis (flowers like glove fingers, a narcotic)—Beauty but too careless, I
am afraid of you.
Dipsacus (a thistle the flowers of which keep the dew) I thirst after you.
Dogrose—Poetry. Spring. Beginning of love. You have enchanted me.
Will you love me ?
Dandelion—Dull jealousy.

LOW MAGIC

E

Easter Daisy—Let us enjoy our youth.
Elderflower—Kindness.
Eucalyptus—Love of travelling.

F

Fennel (aromatic)—What a strong perfume of love !
Fern—Confidence and sincerity. Have faith in me.
Flax—Simplicity, gratitude.
Forget-me-not—Forget me not.
Foxtail—You are spiteful.
Figwood—I shall justify myself.
Fir (twig of)—I am afraid of suffering.
Fuchsia—You are full of attentions, but you are wasting your time.
Fumiter (bitter taste)—You are unkind !

G

Gardenia—I love you in secret.
Gorse—My thoughts for you (or your thoughts for me) are like golden butter-
    flies.
Geranium (white)—you are frank.
Geranium (pink)—You are childish.
Geranium (red)—You are an idiot. (Together—I respect but don't love you).
Glycinia—It is only friendship, but mutual.
Gladiola (swordshaped leaves)—You pierce my heart.
Guelder rose—Slander. Or, I love you less.
Golden rod—Friendly scolding.

H

Hawthorn—Sweet hope. Timid request. You are the queen, the only one.
Helenia—Tears. You are hurting me.
Heliantus—Do not trust to appearances.
Heliotrope—Intoxication of love. I am enchanted.
Hemerocallus (blue)—Perseverance.
Hemerocallus (yellow)—Unfaithfulness.
Henbane—I do not trust you.
Hollyhock—Beauty.
Hellebore (was thought to cure madness)—You are too smart.
Hemlock—Perfidy. Poison. Beware of treachery. And, we must die !
    (In olden times those condemned to death were " allowed to commit
    suicide " by drinking the poison which can be extracted from this).
Honeysuckle—Bond of love. We belong to each other.
Holly—Take care !
Hyacinth (white)—Benevolence. Be good !
Hyacinth (blue)—I have my suspicions.
Hyssop—I am tired of you.
Hydrangea (a beautiful flower without scent)—You are beautiful, but cold.

I

Immortelle—Always yours! (it does not fade).
Ivy—Eternal friendship (or love). I die where I cling.

J

Jasmin (white)—Our love will be so sweet!
Jasmin (yellow)—Our love will be passionate.
Jasmin (red)—Our love will be intoxication, folly.
Jonquil—Violent sympathy. Desire, I die of love.
Julian—You have made a mistake.

L

Laurel (glory)—I shall conquer you.
Laurel rose—It is a mere flirtation.
Lavender—Fervent but silent love.
Lilac (white)—First dream of love.
Lilac (mauve)—Do you still love me?
Lily (white)—Purity.
Lily (tiger)—Pride and wealth.
Lily of the valley—Renewed happiness. Let us make it up.
Laburnum—You have broken my heart.
Larkspur—Read in my heart.
Limetree—It is conjugal love that I want.
Lettuce (plagiarism of the cornflower)—I am disappointed.
Lobelia—Kind thoughts.
Lupin—Need of rest.
Lychnis—Irresistible sympathy.

M

Mandragora—Alas! I am too poor.
Marguerite—Innocence. Do you love me?
Marguerite (China aster)—I shall fight against Fate.
Marjoram—I shall comfort you. Also, free love.
Mallow—Gentle and pure affection.
Marshmallow—You are gentle. Be kind.
Medlar—Be more daring.
Mint—Violent love.
Mimosa—Great daintiness.
Moneywort—I am disinterested.
Moss—Friendship, nothing more.
Myrtle—Love returned, I also love you.
Mignonette—Hidden love. Also, I am modest.
Mistletoe—I surmount everything. I shall conquer.
Marigold—Disquiet. What is the matter with you? (Bad omen).

LOW MAGIC

N

Narcissus—Egotism. Conceit.
Nasturtium—Flame of love. You light it in my heart.
Nenuphar—Coldness. You are made of ice.
Nicotine—The obstacle is overcome.
Nigello—Bonds of love.
Nettle—Cruelty. You break my heart.

O

Olive branch—Reconciliation. The palm of peace.
Orange flower—Virginity. I shall not sin.
Orchid—Magnificence.

P

Poppy (small, sign of sleep)—Rest. I am very quiet.
Poppy (white)—My heart is asleep.
Poppy (black)—I have forgotten you.
Pansy—Think of me as I think of you.
Periwinkle—Sweet memories.
Pimpernel—Own that you are beaten.
Petunia—I am furious. Or, why this anger ?
Prickwood—Your image is engraved on my heart.
Phlox (white)—Proposal of love.
Phlox (blue)—Illusion in love.
Phlox (purple)—Sweet dreams.
Peony—I am ashamed of what I have done (I blush for it).
Planetree—They are lies.
Polygala—They are slandering you (or me).
Potato (flower)—I thank you.
Primula—We are young. Let us love each other !
Plum (flowers)—I remind you of your promises.
Privet—I am on the defensive. Or, you are very young.

R

Rosemary—Exclusive love.
Rhubarb—Don't lose heart.
Reed—I like music (the flute of Pan).
Ragwort—I am humble but proud.
Rose (generally)—How beautiful you are to me. How I love you.
Rose (red)—Desire.
Rose (white)—You are innocent and so charming.
Rose (moss)—We shall love each other much in the country.
Rose (Alpine)—I want to work to win you.
Rose (tea)—Our love will be fruitful.
Rose (wild)—I shall follow you everywhere.
Rose full blown—Early marriage.

Rue (wild)—I like my independence.
Rye—Alas, I am poor.
Rose mellow—Beauty.

S

Strawberry—You are delicious. I want you. Also, you are good.
Snowdrop—Let us hope for better days.
Saffron—I call you back to moderation.
Sagittarius—Break (these definite floral meanings must only be used with very great care).
Sainfoin (oscillating flowers)—I hesitate. And, you misunderstand me.
Sarsaparilla—I offer you atonement.
Soapwort—Sensual love.
Sardonyx—I laugh at you.
Sage—I respect you deeply.
Saxifrage—I am in despair.
Scabious (the flower of widows)—You forsake me. Or, I forsake you.
Solomon's Seal—The secret will be duly kept.
Scolopender—Slander, libel.
Sensitive plant—I am very sensitive. Be careful. Don't hurt me.
Syringa—You intoxicate me.
Sunflower—False virtue. False wealth. Also, my eyes see only you.
Spirea—My will is tenacious.
Stramony—Your charms deceive.
Sycamore (leaves)—I am going away for a time.
Sylvia—Open your heart.

T

Tobacco (flower)—I want to forget.
Tamarind—I am careful. Or, be careful.
Tamaris—Count on my protection.
Thlaspi—I shall comfort you.
Thyme (wild)—You have been thoughtless. You are too careless.
Thyme—On seeing you I am thrilled.
Tuberose—I think of death.
Tulip—You are wonderful!
Tulip (double)—You will succeed. We shall succeed.

V

Valerian—Dissimulation (fatal gift).
Veronica—Our thoughts are in accord.
Verbena—Platonic love.
Vesper flower—These are our last lovely days (Vesper, evening).
Vine (leaves)—You intoxicate me.
Vine (wild)—Poetry, imagination.
Violet—Modesty, simplicity, chastity.

Violet (Parma)—Let me love you.
Violet (double)—I return your love (or your friendship).

Y

Yew—Sorrow, affliction (to give a branch of it).
Yucca—Until death.

Z

Zinnia—Take care.

V

The Symbolism and the Magic of Stones

For the Alchemist everything lives. For the Occultist everything can become symbolical. Do minerals react on the body? In any case we have to-day a metallotherapy, just as we have an electrotherapy, a magnetotherapy and a psychotherapy. Stones live. The pearl loses its water, and is then said to die. In assuming death we also assume life. Besides some scientists definitely claim that there are metallic ferments.

However this may be, in olden times men believed in the virtue of stones, both medical and magic. They found relations between the stones and the stars. They invented a symbolism of stones.

For convenience of reference we give tables showing what these beliefs were.

. . . . . .

TABLE SHOWING THE SYMBOLISM AND VIRTUES OF STONES
(From the Ratnapariksa of Buddhabhatta)
(6th Century B.C.)

Their names.	*Their symbolism.*	*Their virtues.*
The Diamond.	Reconciliation and love.	Makes faithful in undertakings.
The Garnet.	Loyalty and frankness.	Gives sincerity of heart.
The Amethyst.	Happiness, wealth.	Gives courage and keeps from drunkenness.
The Jasper.	Courage and wisdom.	Gives constancy and married happiness.
The Sapphire.	Truth and clear conscience.	Gives repentance for faults committed.
The Emerald.	Hope and faithful love.	Gives knowledge of the future.

Their names.	Their symbolism.	Their virtues.
The Agate.	Prosperity, long life.	Gives health.
The Ruby.	Beauty, daintiness.	Preserves from false friendships.
The Cornelian.	Joy, peace.	Disperses evil thoughts and sorrow.
The Opal.	Prayer, tender love.	Increases faithfulness.
The Topaz.	Eager love.	Stays evil dreams.
The Turquoise.	Courage and hope.	Ensures success in love.
The Olivine.	Innocent pleasures.	Simplicity and modesty.
The Peridot.	Thunderbolt.	Encourages marriage.
The Aquamarine.	Youth and Health.	Ensures constant happiness.

TABLE OF THE PROPERTIES OF STONES (according to Fraya)

Black agate defends against envy and makes athletes invincible.

Red agate defends against the sting of spiders and scorpions, against storm and lightning.

Aquamarine worn as earring brings affection.

Amber as a necklace for children defends them against convulsions.

Amethyst protects against drunkenness and poison if the images of the sun and the moon are engraved on it.

Chrysolith protects against gout and madness, and facilitates searches.

Coral protects against epidemics. It turns pale when a loved person is going to die.

Cornelian protects against ruin and betrayal.

Carbuncle gives self-confidence, constancy and energy.

Hematite gives success in lawsuits.

Jade cures colic and kidney troubles.

Cat's-eye protects against spells and the evil eye.

Onyx soothes nocturnal oppressions and dispels nightmares.

Peridot dispels female betrayal and encourages friendship.

Ruby dispels sadness and love troubles.

Sapphire gives health, preserves the sight, protects chastity.

Sardonyx leads to high position.

Selenite strengthens surrounding sympathies.

Topaz is a talisman against hatred and revenge.

Turquoise protects against danger when travelling.

ANOTHER TABLE OF THE SYMBOLISM OF STONES

Black Agate—Courage.	Hematite—Vivacity.
Red Agate—Calm.	Hyacinth—Faithfulness
Aquamarine—Hope.	Jade—Power.
Magnet—Integrity.	Jet—Mourning.

Amber—Health.
Amethyst—Peace of heart.
Beryl (see Aquamarine).
Chiridion[1]—talisman of love.
Chrysolith[2]—Wisdom.
Chrysoprase[3]—Gaiety.
Coral—Attachment.
Adamant—Tranquillity of soul.
Cornelian[3]—Friendship.
Diamond—Frankness.
Emerald—Faithfulness.
Carbuncle—Assurance.
Garnet—Strength.

Jasper—Joy.
Lapis-lazuli—Ability.
Cat's Eye—Long life.
Onyx—Clearness.
Opal—Confidence.
Peridot—Happiness.
Pearl—Purity.
Ruby—Ardent love.
Sapphire—Innocence.
Sardonyx—Vivacity.
Selenite[4]—Intelligence.
Topaz—Gentleness.
Turquoise—Success.

VI

Symbolism and Influence of Colours

Colour, the daughter of Light, was bound to interest men in olden times, just as shapes, numbers, stones, etc. Fruit is judged by its colour. And also sometimes people. Have we not seen the importance which chiromancers attach to the colour of the hand, or typologers to the colour of the face ? Look at the livid and leaden complexion of the perverted youth, the purple nose of the drunkard, the cadaverous hue of the dying. Distrust pale women, said Balzac. Plants also have their characteristic colours, such as the vivid red of the summer poppy full of sun, the melancholy reds and browns of autumn, the repulsive green of some poisonous plants.

We must not neglect colours. Always they were treated as symbolical. According to Ely Star, moral light corresponds to yellow, intellectual light to blue, the light of instinct to red. Who does not remember the celebrated sonnet which gave a colour to each vowel ? Does not the bull attacking a red cloak denote the fury of a brutal instinct let loose ?

The law of the septenary seems to govern Colour. There are seven principal colours in the visible rainbow.

Colour is taken into account in Therapeutics ; this is an explained fact. As Occultism teaches that everything in Nature which is governed by the same number is also subject to the laws relating to this number, there is a whole *Magic of Colours* into which unfortunately we cannot go in detail, but which is of great interest.

We will merely mention that purple is tonic, and that it is beneficial

---

[1] A kind of Turquoise with black lines.
[2] Both a kind of Agate.
[3] A kind of Topaz.
[4] Also called Moonstone.

to pin a piece of sateen of this colour to a window through which the sun shines so that the effect may be felt on a part of the body which is aching; that red gives heat (Le Clerc, former Benedictine and astrologer to Napoleon I, in his old age never went out without being wrapped in a scarlet cape); that golden yellow calms the nerves and helps inspiration (the Thibetan and Japanese priests and others wear dalmatics of this shade); that blue has electric powers, green has the same powers as the mud baths at Dax, indigo, the brother of water, refreshes; that white gives cheerful thoughts, black dark thoughts.

Let us in conclusion give two more tables :—

A. Zodiacal and planetary relations (founded on the houses of the sky) :—

Ram—Fire.	Libra—Water green.
Taurus—Dark green.	Scorpio—Scarlet.
Gemini—Chestnut.	Sagittarius—Sky blue.
Cancer—Silver.	Capricorn—Black.
Leo—Gold.	Aquarius—Grey.
Virgo—Multi-colour.	Pisces—Navy Blue.
Sun—Gold.	Mars—Red.
Moon—Silver.	Jupiter—Blue.
Mercury—Iridescent.	Saturn—Black.
Venus—Green.	

B. Influences and Virtues (according to Tradition) :—
Colours bringing good luck, symbolic of virtue, are :—

White—Purity, truth, innocent pleasure.
Pink—Morning light, timidity, amiability, welcome.
Blue—Pure love, youth, illusions, moral electricity.
Green—Hope, confidence.
Red—Ardour, health, strength, heat.
Purple—Intelligence, politeness, knowledge, tonic.
Amaranth—Constancy in friendship. Faithfulness in love.
Lilac—Freshness, charm, first love.
Violet mixed with Green and Yellow—Triumph.

Unlucky colours, bringing bad luck, denoting defects are :—

Black—Sorrow, mourning.
Grey—Melancholy, neurasthenia.
Orange—Lust, great heat.
Yellow—Falseness, betrayal, avarice, ambition.[1]

---

[1] Subject to certain reservations. No doubt yellow is the colour of deception in love. But splendid qualities redeem this symbolism. And it is difficult to accept the curse attached to orange, which is but a reddish yellow.

LOW MAGIC

Brown—Repentance, sorrow.
Dead Leaf—Sorrows, ruin.
Purple—Pride. [1]
White edged with Black—Death, tears.

VII

Modern Magic

We have given in the preceding pages, a collection, somewhat mixed perhaps, of old beliefs and magic acts. In the following we will try and give a survey of the remnant of Magic which modern Magicians have thought right to preserve. And the reader will not be astonished at what he will find, however surprising it may be, when he remembers that a part of this remnant has been examined by serious-minded men like Eliphas Lévi, Guaïta, Barlet, Saint-Yves, Papus, Péladan, Piobb, Jagot, etc., and on the other hand that many of these practices which seem so grotesque or diabolic, such as Magic Mirrors, the Casting of Spells, etc., can to-day be produced very scientifically and without the aid of dark infernal spirits.

As we have said, it was by starting with hyperpsychical phenomena (which he himself calls hyperphysical) that Paul Jagot went back to the practices of Magic. We will follow him stage by stage, giving a short account of his labours, and leaving on one side everything that relates to divination, already studied by Guaïta, Barlet, Saint-Yves, Papus, Peladan, Piobb, Jagot, etc. [2]

Great psychical phenomena, he says, arise from the first principles of Magic. And he makes a list of the main ones among them, which either have already been described by us or will be found in our Third Part, that is to say :—

I. *Exteriorisation of Sensitiveness* (experiments by Joire, [3] by Colonel de Rochas, etc.).

II. *Exteriorisation of Motivity* (numerous experiments by Darien, Maxwell, Richet, Rochas, Count Grammont, Baron Watteville, Sabatier, Victorien Sardou, Adolphe Brisson, Camille Flammarion, etc. See Third Part. This deals with phenomena of mediumship such as movements of things, auditions, mysterious shocks, etc.)

[1] Subject to certain reservations. Purple is merely an enhanced red. Briefly, we ought not to put yellow and red with their various shades into this sorrowful list. In our opinion there is no justification for it.

[2] We have chosen P. Jagot's book as the most recent. But it would be advisable also to read the *Treatise of Practical Magic* by Papus (Chacornac—publisher).

[3] Dr. Joire is the President of the Universal Society for Psychical Studies. He wrote *Psychic and supernormal Phenomena, Neuro-Hypnology.* See also *The Mysteries of Hypnosis* by G. de Duborn ; *Modern Scientific Method of Magnetism, Hypnotism, Suggestion,* by P. Jagot, and others.

III. *Metagnomy.* We have spoken of this above. It is the perception of persons, of things, beyond the radius of the senses of the subject, and of past or future events.

IV. *Telepsychics.* These are presentiments which have come true (see Third Part).

V. *Divided Personality.* This is the extraordinary but tested phenomenon of bilocation (see Third Part), whereby a person projects his *ego* to a distance, his body remaining stationary.

Secondly, a list of these to some extent miraculous possibilities having been made, P. Jagot describes, as we shall do later on, the constitution of Man according to Occult Science. This constitution, both in the Universe and in Man, is threefold, in the Cosmos physical, hyperphysical (astral plane, more subtle than matter) and spiritual (first and ruling cause of the other two elements), and in Man (the microcosm) is corporal (the anatomical body), astral (astral body, giving life to the physical organism, and of a subtle substance identical with that of the astral plane) and mental (the mental body is a conscious, intelligent and indestructible entity).

Starting with these twofold data we may conclude :—

That there exists between the Universe and Man a threefold relation owing to which Man is able to act by other than bodily means (as is believed by materialists who deny both the astral body, cosmic or human, and the spiritual world, ruler of the Universe, or in Man his immortal *ego*).

The Occultist (and consequently the Magician) looks upon the physical body merely as a *temporary support* of the astral and mental human being. The astral being directs our organic, emotional and intellectual activities, enters into and closely blends with the physical body, presides over the cellular life, the building and maintenance of the individual being, orders his vegetative life and, as the centre of the subconscious, relates sensations and impressions received by the senses. The mental being, still more subtle, enters into the astral and the physical being, gives consciousness and stimulates the brain ; it is the seat of thought, of will-power, of the psychic faculties ; it rules the complete individual. In one word, where the classic psychologist sees three centres in the same body—sensation, feeling, thought —the occultist sees three distinct principles.

In order to explain this occult constitution of Man, Hector Durville has devised a very apt comparison. Imagine a large hole filled with stones. These stones represent matter and its various states. It is the physical state (either of the Cosmos or of Man). But these stones leave larger or smaller interstices between them which you may fill up, with sand for instance. This sand represents the astral (astral plane or astral body). Finally even this sand can still let water pass between its grains. This water is the spiritual of the Cosmos, the mental in Man.

This at once explains telepathy and clairvoyance, since the astral plane binds together all human beings, at whatever distance from each other they may be.

The astral body has been variously termed *fluid body* by Dr. Baraduc, *enormon* by Hippocrates, *perisprit* by Allan Kardec, *luminous body* by Pythagoras, *ethereal body* by the Greeks, *body glorious* by the Church. This diversity of names make the unity of belief still more distinct.

Let us remark in passing that *all religions and all metaphysics* have known this threefold aspect of man. So that we do not know which is to surprise us more, either materialistic Science which denies all this documentary evidence, or the Christian Church which forgets what it formerly believed.

The following table is convincing :—

Egypt :—Khat (body), Ka (double or astral), Khou (intellect).
China :—Xuong (organic body), Khi (breath of life), Whun (will).
Persia :—Djan (body and life), Ferouer (substance), Akkho (eternal principle).
Greece :—Body, Shadow, Mind.
India :—Rupa (physical body), Kama Roupa (body or desire), Atmat (mind).
Israel :—Gouph (body), Nephesch and Ruach (soul), Neschamah (pure spirit).
Primitive Christianity :—Corpus, Anima, Spiritus.

The necessary relations will easily be made. The differences are mere shades. St. Thomas himself distinguished three kinds of soul.

Some schools, however, go so far as to count five elements in man, and others seven. All they do is to subdivide the above mentioned three fundamental elements. For instance, in the case of divided personality, the physical body must continue to have an animator of its cells. Advanced Occultists call this animator the *etheric double*. There are supersensitives who see it in graveyards soon after the burial of the corpse from which it frees itself (to this are due many tales of ghosts). It is this etheric double which is influenced by magnetisers to restore the health of their patients.

So also the mental body presupposes a *causal body* which affects the moral or constitutional consciousness, some philosophers holding this to be different from the psychological consciousness.

Thus we have five elements. Esoteric Buddhism suggests two more, corresponding to two states of the soul which are very rare but said to have been proved, that is, the *Buddhistic body* (the identification of the *ego* with the Universal Being) and the *athmic body* (or pure spirit, the perceptive centre of primal causes). Stanislas de Guaïta and many theosophists recognise this septenary.

. . . . .

For each of our principles, concludes P. Jagot (who confines himself to the ternary), we are therefore in relation with the three planes of the Universe—the plane of realities, the plane of virtualities and the plane of directions. With our physical senses we apprehend matter; through the astral body we are bathed in a cosmic ocean (the astral plane) identical with our astral essence, and are thus in contact with our fellow-beings and with the forces, agents and entities whose inter-play determines the genesis of facts; through the mental body we are in touch with causes.

This explains the power of Thought, producing invisible vibrating waves which try to translate themselves into realities. These forces become the conductors of elements which are analogous to them, and they put into motion the plan of virtualities where events *are in prepara-tion.* Hence the *creative* force of Thought, proved by the photographs of Dr. Baraduc and Commandant Darget, who have succeeded in fixing on the sensitive plate the effort of the mental body.[1] Thoughts thus become real *material* things as well as *forces.* An Englishman, Richard Ingalese[2] goes so far as to assert that by addressing mentally, in a concrete form, a request to the Universal Consciousness (astral and mental plane) we can obtain from the latter the object thought of, because in some way we project the *matrix* of the thing which we evoked. The whole of the remarkable passage of Paul Jagot as to the method of *commanding our fate* should be read, where he proves that a psychic who is awake and strong *can do everything he wants to,*[3] and that he has an influence not only on other persons, but also *on events.*

The practice of this individual psychism is *Personal Magic,* which corresponds to the first two methods mentioned above by Pierre Piobb for the use of fluids.

. . . . .

Side by side with this personal Magic we have *Traditional Magic,* which is much more complicated, and which is in the main the Magic of which we have spoken in our " Storehouse of Low Magic." We repeat that we attach no derogatory meaning to this expression, since P. Piobb also calls it High Magic. It is simply that we have kept the

---

[1] See his *Transcendental Photography,* where will be found what are called *sign-manuals* of the soul. See also *Personal Magnetism,* by Hector Durville.

[2] See his *History and Power of Thought.*

[3] *Treatise of Occult Sciences and Practical Magic,* page 54 et seq.

latter term for Hermetic Philosophy, but we admit that the expression is incorrect, and explain it by the convenience of language.

For the practice of this difficult Magic we require a material, a locality and very special gifts.

The first thing required to be thoroughly known here is elementary Astrology; a chapter at the beginning of this book deals with this, to which we refer the reader, so that he may be thoroughly familiar with the influence of each of the seven planets, as each one of them assists, to the exclusion of all others, in the different magical operations.

Thus it is necessary to know, with the assistance of the almanacs of Raphael, the position of the various planets in the Zodiac and their aspect on each day of the year, especially the position and aspect of the Moon (beneficent when it is increasing, maleficent when it is decreasing), the influence dominating each day of the week (the Sun on Sunday, the Moon on Monday, etc.) and each hour of the day (see the table).

The particular realm of each planet should also be remembered :—

The Sun—Influence favourable to acts relating to active vitality (knowledge, position, love, etc.)

The Moon—Influence favourable to acts relating to vegetative activity (security, foreknowledge, journeys, etc.)

Mars—Influence favourable to combativeness (domination, industry, surgery, etc.)

Mercury—Influence favourable to adaptiveness (skill, commerce, medicine, diplomacy, etc.)

Jupiter—Influence favourable to social position (the family, comfort, great opportunities, etc.)

Venus—Influence favourable to physical perfection (harmony, charm, art, average luck.)

Saturn—Influence favourable to long life, to abstract science (mines, treasures, hidden knowledge, etc.)

In order to attract the influence of the entities presiding over the functions of the Cosmos and to capture the hyperphysical forces the following are used :—

1. Names, signs, figures, the writing of which exercises a special conductive power over the astral.
2. Substances from the three kingdoms, the properties of which harmonise with the influences.

Mr. Jagot gives in this connection seven tables[1] which we reproduce here, and which show, starting at the top :—

[1] These tables derive from the kabbalistic Astrology included in the *Treatise of Practical Magic* of Papus, already referred to.

1. A synthetic design of the entities in touch with the planet and its place in the Zodiac.
2. The general design of the vibratory tonality of the planet.
3. The sign which raises the entity presiding over the beneficent acts of the planet.
4. The sign which raises the entity presiding over the maleficent acts of the planet.
5. A kabbalistic table of figures.

These signs and designs should be reproduced on metal or parchment as the case may be.

Sun

Metal :—Gold.
Colour :—Golden yellow.
Minerals :—Amber, chrysolith, carbuncle, hyacinth, topaz.
Plants :—Angelica, balsam, corn, cinnamon, cardamon, caron, celandine, common cabbage, chrysanthemum, cyclamen, gentian, clove tree, heliotrope, laurel, lavender, lotus, marjoram, pimpernel, orange tree, barley, palm-tree, primula, buttercup, polygonium, rosemary, saffron, red sandalwood, sage, tansy, thyme.
Animals :—Eagle, goat, ram, canary, condor, falcon, ibis, lion, parrot.
Synthetic perfume :—Red sandalwood.
Compound perfume :—Equal quantities of saffron, aloe wood, balm, laurel seed, cloves, myrrh, incense, musk, ambergris. According to tradition the above substances should be made into a paste before being reduced to powder, and they should be burnt, as is generally done, with incense or benzoin, and the blood of the animals mentioned above.

Moon

Metal :—Silver.
Colour :—Silvery or white.
Minerals :—Beryl, diamond, crystal, opal, mother-of-pearl.
Plants :—Crab-apple, hay, camphor, cucumber, poppy, pumpkin gourd, lettuce, melon, nenuphar, water-melon, purslane, rampion, beetroot, reed, white sandalwood, tamaris, limetree.
Animals :—Frog, toad, crab, cat, osprey, bat, goose, swan, hare, rabbit, nightingale.
Synthetic perfume :—Aloe.
Compound perfume :—Equal quantities of seed of white poppy, storax, benzoin, powdered camphor, frog's head, bull's eye. The paste must be prepared with goose blood.

LOW MAGIC

Mars

Metal :—Iron.
Colour :—Red.

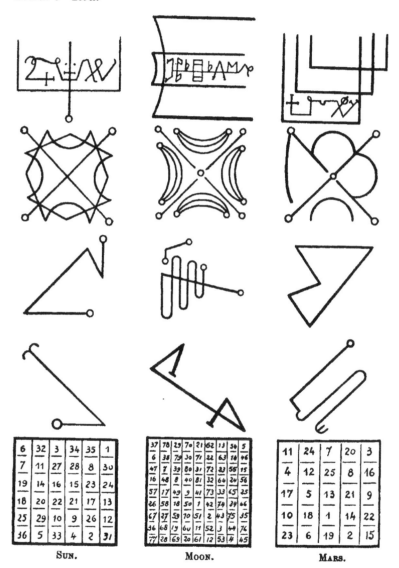

6	32	3	34	35	1
7	11	27	28	8	30
19	14	16	15	23	24
18	20	22	21	17	13
25	29	10	9	26	12
36	5	33	4	2	31

SUN.

37	78	29	70	21	62	13	54	5
6	38	79	30	71	22	63	14	46
47	7	39	80	31	72	23	55	15
16	48	8	40	81	32	64	24	56
57	17	49	9	41	73	33	65	25
26	58	18	50	1	42	74	34	66
67	27	59	10	51	2	43	75	35
36	68	19	60	11	52	3	44	76
77	28	69	20	61	12	53	4	45

MOON.

11	24	7	20	3
4	12	25	8	16
17	5	13	21	9
10	18	1	14	22
23	6	19	2	15

MARS.

Minerals :—Ruby, bloodstone, natural magnet, hematite, jasper, garnet.

Plants :—Absinthe, acanthus, wild celery, agaric, garlic, wormwood, artichoke, arum, asparagus, burdock, basil, belladonna, briar, bryony, hemp, thistle, cibol, colocinth, bull's horn, cornel-tree, garden-cress, dog's-tongue, euphrasy, bean, fern, gorse, gladiola, woad, hore-hound, mint, mustard, nutmeg, onion, auricula, nettle, poppy, leek, pepper-tree, blackthorn, horse-radish, wallflower, rhubarb, veronica, vine.

Animals :—Tiger, jaguar, panther, kite, cock, green woodpecker, horse, wolf, boar, dog, hawk, scorpion, spider.

Synthetic perfume :—Briar.

Compound perfume :—Equal quantities of spurge, cornel, ammonia, root of hellebore, powdered magnet, sulphur, gentian root.

Make into a paste with the blood of one of the animals corresponding to Mars, or in default of this with blood of any butcher's animal.

Mercury

Metal :—Mercury.

Colour :—Any shot neutral colour.

Minerals :—Sardonyx, cornelian, agate, chalcedony.

Plants :—Acacia, aniseed, beet, camomile, honeysuckle, chicory, couch-grass, Milan kale, filbert-tree, wild rose, endive, madder, juniper, marshmallow, matricaria, mercury, yarrow, millet, hazelnut, sorrel, cinquefoil, sarsaparilla, savory, scabious, elder, tea, clover, privet, valerian.

Animals :—Cat (already given as belonging to the moon, but doubly owned), fox, magpie, swallow, monkey, linnet, weasel, thrush, bee, ant, common green lizard.

Synthetic perfume :—Mastic resin.

Compound perfume :—Equal quantities of mastic, incense, cloves, cinquefoil, powdered agate, to be made into a paste with the blood of one of the animals mentioned above, preferably a fox.

Jupiter

Metal :—Tin.

Colour :—Blue.

Minerals :—Sapphire, amethyst, turquoise, jasper, diamond with green or blue reflection.

Plants :—Agrimony, aloe, amaranth, rest-harrow, daisy, beetroot, borage, bugloss, cedar, centaury, cherry tree, charm, red cabbage, quince, colchicum, sorb-apple, barberry, white fig tree, strawberry, germander, flax, mulberry, elm tree, poplar, peony, plane tree, plum tree, buckwheat, sesame, violet.

Animals :—Buck, stag, giraffe, lark, partridge.   Jupiterian animals are known by the peaceful, majestic, stately gait.

Synthetic perfume :—Saffron.

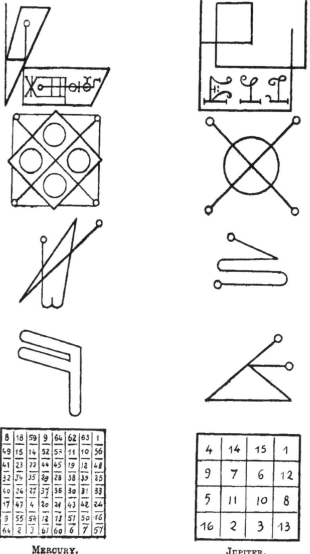

8	18	59	9	64	62	63	1
49	15	14	52	53	11	10	56
41	23	22	44	45	19	12	48
32	34	35	29	28	38	39	25
40	26	27	37	36	30	31	33
17	47	4	20	21	43	42	24
9	55	54	12	13	51	50	16
64	2	3	61	60	6	7	57

MERCURY.

4	14	15	1
9	7	6	12
5	11	10	8
16	2	3	13

JUPITER.

Compound perfume :—Equal parts of seeds of ash, aloe wood, storax, benzoin, powdered azurite, powdered peacock feathers. Mix into a paste with the blood of a partridge.

Venus

Metal :—Copper.

Colour :—Green.

Minerals :—Emerald, light coral, sapphire with pink reflections.

Plants :—Almond tree, box, cassia, celandine, honeysuckle, lemon-tree, coriander, watercress, spinach, fuchsia, clover, mistletoe, iris, hyacinth, house-leek, purple lilac, lily, cherry-pie, medlar, forget-me-not, myrtle, easter daisy, pansy, periwinkle, plantain, apple tree, mignonette, rose, satyrion, wild thyme, colt's-foot, verbena.

Animals :—Turtledove, nightingale, wood-pigeon, dove, pigeon, goat, sheep, sparrow, pheasant, butterflies.

Synthetic perfume :—Musk.

Compound perfume :—Equal proportions of musk, ambergris, aloe wood, red roses, powdered coral, to be made into a paste with the blood of one of the above animals, preferably a dove.

Saturn

Metal :—Lead.

Colour :—Black.

Minerals :—Obsidian, onyx, jet, diamond and black coral.

Plants :—Aconite, agnus-castus, asphodel, cactus, hemlock, cocoa, cummin, cypress, datura, hellebore, spurge, fennel, black fig, male fern, stavesacre, lichen, mandragora, moss, parietary, lungwort, rue, soapwort, weeping willow, saxifrage, scrofulary, serpentine, tobacco plant.

Animals :—Vulture, owl, toad (already mentioned, but doubly owned), bat, great-owl, little owl, mole.

Synthetic perfume :—Sulphur.

Compound perfume :—Equal parts of seed of black poppy, seed of henbane, root of mandragora, powdered magnetic iron, powdered myrrh, made into a paste with the blood of one of the above named animals, preferably a bat.

. . . . . .

The making of Talismans.—As has been seen above, in order to make a talisman it is necessary first of all to know what results are to be obtained, then, knowing this, to capture the required influence by the use of the signs, figures and substances which give the greatest intensity, remembering to take the relative times into account. And at once two observations suggest themselves :—

LOW MAGIC

1. The absolute uselessness of the fetishes, amulets, luck-bringers, etc., sold in the shops.
2. The necessity, in order to make a talisman useful, that it shall be manufactured by its wearer or by a third party interested in the wearer, who shall make it *for his use.*

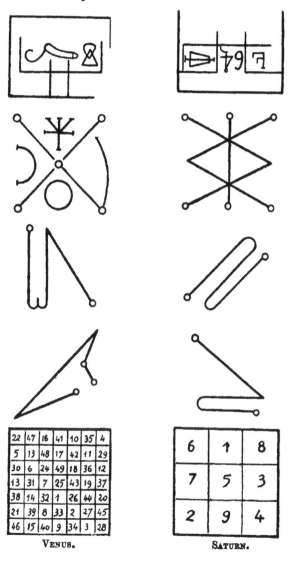

VENUS. SATURN.

How is it to be made ? By referring to the information given above, or by using a complete ritual such as that quoted by Piobb (*Formulary of High Magic*), by Papus, or by Jagot (*Treatise of Occult Sciences*, already referred to).

For instance, is it desired to make a solar talisman in order to capture harmonies favourable to spiritual, intellectual and material improvement, to artistic fame, to success with women, to a vivifying of the heart ? You must have a disc of yellow gold, some yellow silk, a new paintbrush, a carbuncle, portions of solar plants or animals, solar perfume and an incense burner. At the correct time (a Sunday, or when the Sun passes through the constellation of Leo in a good aspect, and in any case at the hour of the Sun) you withdraw into a room with yellow hangings, burn the appropriate perfume, engrave on one side of the disc the figured table of the Sun, on the other ·side the appropriate signs (see the table of the Septenary), then enclose the disc together with the stone (carbuncle) and the suitable packets of plant and animal matter (see the table) in a bag of yellow material sewn with a thread of the same colour.

The method is the same with the other planetary talismans.

Evocations.—Evocation is the calling up of the entities which seem to direct the cosmic forces in the astral and other planes, or superior beings called *elementals*,[1] who animate the four fundamental elements (earth, water, air, fire). But there is another not very thoroughly identified hierarchy of elementals which inhabit the Invisible. The evocation calls them up or conjures them, according to whether they are good or evil, and in various ways captures or commands them. But this is a difficult and sometimes dangerous proceeding, impossible for the weak or the supersensitive. It requires a very thorough knowledge of the complicated rites of which the Treatise of Mr. Jagot, and even the book of Papus, give but a summary, and which we shall not attempt to set out in this elementary Encyclopædia.

Modern Black Magic.—If we consider Magic with the knowledge of the possibility of phenomena founded on the occult principles above set forth, and at the same time with the wish of avoiding any extra-scientific exaggeration, we shall arrive at a better understanding of the practices of modern witchcraft which have no connection whatever with demoniac agency.

No doubt there still are sorcerers, but they may be looked upon as magicians of the second rank, and according to the very apt comparison of Papus, may be put into the same position as that occupied by a workman compared with his engineer working in the same class of industry. The engineer, trained in his College, has much more

[1] See the very remarkable pages of Papus on *Elementals* in his *Treatise of Practical Magic*, page 401 et seq. Also see his book and the writings of Eliphas Lévi on Evocations.

theoretical knowledge and much less practical experience; the work-man has much more manual skill, but lacks technical knowledge. So it is in the case of the sorcerer compared with the magician, at any rate with the modern magician who is more a scientist of the psychical laboratory (for the ancient magician often combined an immense knowledge with a constant practice rendered easy by faith around him). The sorcerer of to-day, the village sorcerer, the sorcerer of savage tribes, is above all an empirical experimenter who uses given occult methods without knowing their laws.

But some sorcerers are honest people, who try by the exercise of their psychic gifts to relieve the sufferings of their neighbours; they are healers, bonesetters, intuitives who have learnt certain secrets of Nature and understand simples (we mean by this wild medicinal plants). Others, less honest, indiscriminately work good or evil for money, or to satisfy the passions of others or their own, here giving a good prescription, there casting an evil spell. They are the most numerous, for human nature, alas, consists mainly of people in whom both Good and Evil have their dwelling. Finally there are the frank scoundrels, who work only for hatred, destruction and death, those who tie knots, the jettatores, poisoners, who invent the worst spells. They are to be feared, and are, unfortunately, *actually maleficent.*

The sorcerer generally begins as an odd youth, sickly, mocked by his comrades, bearing the triple sign-manual of Saturn, Mars and Mercury in bad aspect, sometimes with an additional sign-manual of the Moon, seeking solitude where his intuition increases, seeking also the company of some other sorcerer of the neighbourhood whose secret knowledge he tries to purchase from an obscure design to avenge himself on Fate by hidden methods of rule.

Then the little sorcerer exerts himself, finds intuitively old formulæ in books of spells, or manages to understand those which his teacher hands on to him, he is able more or less correctly to use magnetism, suggestion, ordinary magic. If at bottom he is honest, he will be content with this. If not, he will try to go farther, and eventually tries his hand at the raising of demons.

The true magician, says Jagot, has a well trained will and possesses the four conditions of success :—clearness of the mental representation of the aim to be attained, continuity of such representation, complete concentration of mental energy and intensity of volition. The sorcerer, who is without this great discipline, tries to reach obsession by a stimulant, maintains it by a series of awkward and grotesque rites, manages to concentrate his attention by looking fixedly at certain objects for a long time, finally reaches exaltation by reciting with full faith formulæ which he has learnt by heart. Thus, consciously or not, he gets into a vibratory condition which enables him to act.

But what acts can he perform ?

He is quite obviously able to magnetise various substances to an extent which entails good or evil results for human beings, animals, or the harvest, he can influence some people by tele-psychics, haunt a house by projecting his astral body, obsess, frighten, act by suggestion, cure ills, but also make them worse, cast spells. And weak and impressionable persons fall an easy prey to him, also excitable people in the periods of depression which invariably follow on outbursts of temper, also those who, bearing a grudge, and desiring with all their power calamities for their enemies, succeed in acting as continual conductors of evil influences. The sorcerer attracts, sustains and projects elementals and larvæ in order to disturb normal conditions. He may even become able, through his own powers, to bring about phenomena of mediumship (see Third Part) and to consolidate the exteriorisation of his double into a material-isation which may take a truly diabolical shape if his over-excited imagination so wills it.

The sorcerer moves the astral plane which bathes not only humans, but all beings, even inorganic. Matter lives, and the atom evolves (we have spoken of gamahés). If there is life in minerals, *d fortiori* there must be life in plants, and intelligent life in animals. " The power of the tamer over the wild beast," says Paul Jagot, " the animosity of the police dog against the criminal, the sagacity which dogs have shown in recognising, holding and denouncing the murderer of their master, their lugubrious howling if there is a corpse in the neighbourhood, the conductive thread of the homing pigeon, all these can be explained through *the astral body* of the animal."

It is because he acts on the astral plane that the sorcerer is able to kill domestic animals, to sterilise the harvest, to harm a man's health at a distance, to cause mental trouble, to cast spells, even to " cast the evil eye," so great is his power over the timid.

We could not better close these remarks on modern witchcraft and its possibilities than by quoting two cases recorded in the reports, quoting from Mr. Paul Jagot, who will forgive us for borrowing, in this part of our chapter, so much from his *Treatise of Occult Sciences and Practical Magic*, one of the most remarkable, clear and fascinating books on these matters which we have seen, and which we strongly recommend to our readers in order to complete their knowledge of the conceptions of Magic which we are compelled to condense in an encyclopædia in which we have to deal with so many other matters.

The first of these events was reported by Stanislas de Guaïta, the second by Mirville.

A man of the name of Hocque, a shepherd, was sentenced to the Galleys by the High Court of Pacy on the 2nd September, 1687, for having, as public report had it, cast a spell on cattle. Hocque in vain appealed against the sentence of the Bailiff, and whilst he was still in prison the suggestion was made that he should be given a companion of the name of Beatrix, who was no more and no less than what we to-day call a copper's nark. Beatrix succeeded in making Hocque talk, and the latter in fact confessed that he had buried a dose of poison in a stable, and that the epidemic would stop if the charm was destroyed. Beatrix makes a report of the conversation, and he is told again to make the culprit drink and to obtain from him the breaking of the spell. Which was done. Hocque fell into the trap, forgetting the dire magic law of the shock on the rebound of which we have already spoken and which operates the return of the current, deflected from its objective, to its starting point with redoubled force. And the sorcerer wrote a letter to ask a colleague in Burgundy to raise the curse. But as soon as the messenger had started, he returned to his senses ; he saw his error, became furious with the traitor and tried to strangle him. He was stopped in time, and meanwhile the sorcerer in Burgundy carried out his task. But as soon as he had burnt the poison, the colleague showed great sorrow at having done so, for he then learnt, no doubt by telepathy, since he did not know it before, that the author of the spell was in Paris, in prison, and that he would pay with his life for this broken magic. And in fact at the same hour Hocque was dying in remarkable convulsions and like one possessed.

The documents proving this strange trial are in the Central Office of the High Court.

The following deals with a haunted house. It dates back to 1851, and took place in Cideville, in the Seine-Inférieure.

A shepherd of the name of Thorel (shepherds seem to be particularly adept at witchcraft) was accused by his master and teacher, a sorcerer like himself, and denounced by the priest of Cideville, of striking the latter by occult means to avenge himself. But the priest seems to have been fairly immune from such attacks, and in his turn he prosecuted Thorel before the Courts. The latter then attacked one of the pupils of the priest with such success that the presbytery was soon haunted ; the walls shook, unexplainable noises occurred, the furniture moved of itself, in short nothing was lacking. The authorities, the Mayor, the Judge, the physician, all certified the facts. Better still, the be-witched boy saw Thorel's *double*, and even this spectre attacked him to such an extent that the marks of the blows remained visible. A priest who was brought in as witness and was well versed in occult practices, knowing the dissolving action of a steel point on the coagulated fluid, took an appropriate tool and threw it in the direction of the spectre. Immediately a flame burst forth, smoke invaded the room, and a voice asked that this hyperpsychic duel should end. The priestly victor requested that the culprit should come and ask the forgiveness of his victim. And on the morrow, under the influence of this powerful suggestion, Thorel himself came to the presbytery. But this time he tried to strike the vicar of Cideville, who threatened him with his stick. The Justice of the Peace of Yerville was present. As previous to these proceedings Thorel had brought an action against the priest for damages, he was non-suited and ordered to pay the costs. The whole matter with the depositions and evidence is preserved in the judicial archives of Yerville.

Here also we have a case of divided personality. This coming out of the astral may also explain the various stories of werewolves, as some very expert sorcerers were able to alter the shape of their double, and also the Sabbath, where the double of some initiate might well actually take the shape of the traditional Satan. But Gassendi suggests yet another possibility. One day he succeeded in obtaining from the sorcerer information as to the means by which he went to the Sabbath. The sorcerer took certain drugs, rubbed himself with a narcotic ointment and at once fell into a heavy sleep, on awaking from which he asked the physician, whom he thought he had taken with him, if he had thoroughly enjoyed himself amongst the devils, telling him of the scenes at which he was quite sure he had been present !

. . . . . .

We were going to finish here with our tales of Witchcraft, when the remarkable volume of Ely Star, *Mysteries of Beings*, fell into our hands, and we cannot refrain from quoting the following facts vouched for by the author :—

The explorer Saint Pol Lias told him that one day, when he was on a mission in Kaffraria, he saw a negro who was going to be executed because he " made wood speak," in other words because he practised witchcraft.

" Is it possible ? " asked Saint Pol, and asked for proof.

" Give me your stick," said the negro, and taking it in his hand, he rubbed it, uttering at the same time barbaric and no doubt magical words, then gave it back, saying, " And now you may stick it in the earth and question it, it will answer you."

Whereupon the negro returned to his place amidst the soldiers and went to his death humming some war song.

Saint Pol went off saddened and intrigued, first of all sceptical, then driven by curiosity he turned into a little oasis where, half an hour later, he tried the experiment.

Having planted the stick in the earth, he asked :

" Spirit of the Wood, will you answer me ? "

" Yes," uttered a thin and distant voice, which he at first took for an acoustic illusion.

However, not afraid of being laughed at, as there was no one near him, he put two definite questions as to the time of arrival in port of a boat which he expected, and as to the presence of a certain person who ought to have been among the passengers.

And the thin little voice gave him the information he wanted.

" You may believe me if you like," concluded Saint Pol in telling the story to Ély Star, " but the details were exact."

" What do you think of it ? "

" I think that I believe in everything, that I doubt of everything, and that I do not deny anything."

" There speaks a wise man. And did the stick make further prophecies ? "

" No, for by the time I questioned it again, the unfortunate sorcerer must have been executed."

How is this phenomenon to be explained ? Perhaps by supposing, as is suggested by Jagot, that the Kaffir sorcerer was able to exteriorise his double and even his voice whilst remaining in psychical contact with the explorer, thus following him into the oasis and from a distance replying to his questions.

Another traveller, A.D., quoted by Ely Star, has told of the marvels worked by sorcerers of Dahomey and Madagascar, who are sometimes as powerful in magic as the Indian Fakirs. One of them (in Dahomey) one day told A.D. that he possessed a terrible curse, and as the traveller did not believe him, he said :

" Point out a tree to me, and I will kill it."

A.D. indicated a small mangrove tree. The sorcerer stretched out his left hand towards the shrub, concentrated his will, and to his amazement the traveller saw the leaves turn yellow and curl up ; at the end of a few minutes the tree was dead.

It is by the opposite power that Fakirs have been seen to make plants germinate and grow in a few minutes, by placing their hands on them.

Father Huc has brought similar tales back from Thibet. He was walking with a bonze when the latter, listening suddenly, told him that he was being called to a Convent far enough away for the journey there and back to take several days.

" Do not worry, however," said the Bonze, " I shall be back here presently, or at least before sunset."

And as the Jesuit appeared surprised, the Bonze continued :

" It is not with my visible body that I shall go yonder, but with my astral body."

" But since you have the power, why do you not simply send your spirit there ? "

" Because it is my *real presence* that is needed there, for a ceremony."

Back in his cell, the Hindu priest made his ablutions, recited his mantrams, then lay down on a mat where he lost consciousness. And whilst his body, stiff in a cataleptic trance, remained stretched out, his double made the journey, going like an arrow to the place where he was expected, and returning less than two hours later.

One of the most astounding Hindu magicians whom Europe knew, thanks to Louis Jacolliot, who brought back from India a volume of the most amazing tales ever heard, was Covindaswamy, of whom a wealthy American relates the following :—

Whilst living at Lahore (the ancient Aagala) the American called Covindaswamy to his hotel to amuse his guests at a big reception.

" What new thing are you going to show us to-night," he asked.

" Let me have that child," said the Fakir, pointing to a baby of two.

He placed the child on some cushions, squatted down in a corner of the room and, covering himself with a shawl, remained a long time without moving. Suddenly the baby got up, dropped its rattle, looked quietly at the assembled guests, cleared its throat, and proceeded to give in absolutely correct language an amazing lecture on one of the most abstruse problems of transcendental philosophy. Then, bowing, it gravely sat down again. The mother, weeping with emotion, went towards the child, which picked up its rattle and resumed its natural expression. Meanwhile the Fakir rose and slowly returned to his place near the host.

We do not think that we have here a simple instance of ventriloquism. By a mighty effort the magician had undoubtedly filled the child with his own will and his own mind.

In 1898, it having been decided to carry out some public works in a certain town in India, a small pagoda had to be demolished. The workmen having found a subterranean crypt, the managing engineer found a sarcophagus and called a bonze to open it, thinking it might contain a mummy.

" No," said the priest, after having examined it, " That is merely a sleeping man."

" Impossible ! " said the engineer.

" Yes," maintained the bonze. " In certain conditions it was possible for our people of old to be buried without dying, and having duly prepared and purified themselves, they could resist decomposition. You will see the proof of what I say."

Some days later the Sacred Council of a Lamaist Convent near by met solemnly and carried out the rites necessary to awaken the sleeping man. They succeeded after about twelve hours of labour and prayers, the presiding priest having massaged the sternum and the forehead of the supposed mummy who at last arose, and a week later was going about like any other person. He had slept for *twenty-two centuries* (this was proved by an examination of the papyrus found with him).

We leave it to the reader to make what hè likes of this fantastic tale which is crowned by an epilogue still more fabulous :—Bored by his surroundings, the ancient Sleeper said, at the end of two years, that he wanted to go away. He called a meeting of the bonzes, clothed himself in a white lambskin, girded himself with a rope, pronounced his spells, and sharply threw the end of the cord into the air ; the rope became taut as if pulled by invisible hands and raised the fakir who ascended mysteriously and disappeared—like Elijah, and like Christ.

. . . . . .

Since we are speaking of Lamaist Convents, let us refer to the recent book of Ossendowski, " *Beasts, Men and Gods*," which has been much attacked as being a skilful mixture of facts (the author has actually been in Mongolia), travellers' tales and fancy. This novel has been compared (in particular by Mr. Borie in an article in the *Mercure de France*) with the tales of Father Huc of which we have just spoken, and who visited Thibet from 1844 to 1846. We will therefore quote the following very curious tale :—

A lama had cut himself open, taken out his entrails and placed them in front of him, and then had returned to his former condition. However horrible and disgusting this sight may be, it is none the less very common in the Lamaist Convents of Tartary. The *Bokte* who is about " to show forth his power " as the Mongolians say, prepares himself for this appalling deed by long days of fasting and prayer. During this time he must abstain from all communication with other men and keep the most absolute silence. When the appointed day comes, the vast multitude of pilgrims meets in the great courtyard of the Convent, and an altar is erected before the door of the temple. At last the *Bokte* appears. He advances solemnly amidst the acclamations of the crowd, sits down on the altar, and takes from his belt a large knife which he places on his knees. At his feet numerous lamas sitting in a circle, begin the terrible invocations of this horrible ceremony. As the prayers proceed the *Bokte* is seen to shake in all his limbs, and gradually to fall into frantic convulsions. The lamas soon lose all restraint ; their voices get louder, their chants become disordered, and finally the saying of prayers gives way to screams and howling. Then the *Bokte* suddenly throws off the scarf which covers him, takes off his vest, grasps the sacred knife and cuts himself open. Whilst the blood is flowing, the multitude prostrates itself before the ghastly sight, and the frenzied *Bokte* is questioned as to hidden things and future events. His replies are looked upon as oracles.

When the devout curiosity of the numerous pilgrims has been satisfied, the lamas return with calm and solemnity to the recital of their prayers. The *Bokte* collects with his right hand some of the blood of his wound, breathes on it three times and throws it in the air with a great shout. He rapidly passes his hand over his wound, and everything returns to its former state without the least trace remaining of this diabolic operation, except perhaps an extreme lassitude.

VIII

Little Supplementary Lexicon of Magic

It being, as we have said above, impossible for us within the restricted scope of this Encyclopædia to go lengthily into detail as to everything concerning magic science, our readers may be grateful to us for giving them briefly various names and information for which we have been unable previously to find a place. We give them in alphabetical order.

A

A.—Letter of bad omen amongst the Greeks. With it the Magicians began the threats made in the name of the Gods.

Abans.—Spirits of the iron mines (Persia).

Abizendegani.—Fountain of water which makes immortal (East). Its Western equivalent—the fountain of Youth.

Abracadabra.—Kabbalistic word of healing which was worn round the neck engraved on a disc on which the letters forming this word were placed on the points of a magic triangle.

Abraxas.—Magic word the seven letters of which make the number 365. In Persian it denotes God.

Acham.—The Demon of Thursday.

Acqua Toffana.—Subtle poison invented of Toffana of Palermo who also made acquata (with probably a basis of arsenic).

Adytum.—Sacred spot in the temples, whence the oracles came.

Agathomedon.—Familiar spirit of the Greeks who drank a glass of wine in his honour after meals.

Agrippa of Wittesheim.—Famous German occult chemist and physician (1486-1535).

Agyrtes.—Priest of Cybele who cast horoscopes.

Akasa.—In esoteric Buddhism this word indicates the organic electricity of stars and human beings.

Akhim.—City of Great Magicians in the Thebaid.

Albumazar.—Astrologer of the 9th century.

Alleur.—Spirit or ghost of ruins (Normandy).

Alrinach.—Demon of Shipwrecks.

Alyssus.—Fountain in Arcadia which cured madness.

Alocer.—Demon in Astrology.

Alminga.—Water plant of the Amazon with which the Indians used to rub their virile member so as to develop it, calling the while on the Gods of fertility.

Amphiaraus.—The most famous soothsayer of old Greece.

Any.—The presiding Demon of Hell.

Anamalech.—The Demon of bad news.

Andras.—The Demon of discord.

Andriagne.—Griffon believed to be ridden by magicians.

Angat.—Name of the Devil in Madagascar. The *Angatos* are ghosts.

Annachiel.—The Spirit of Sagittarius.

Anneberg.—The German Demon of Mines.

Annocchiatura.—Charm by the eyes or by words, the mysterious power of which brings the opposite of the wish (Corsica).

Aour.—Hebrew name for well balanced astral light.

Apone.—Healing fountain in the neighbourhood of Padua. The dwelling place of the oracle Geryon.

Apophrados.—Unlucky days among the Greeks.

Apotelesmatic.—Another mediæval name for Astrology.

Aquiel.—The Demon of Sunday.

Arachula.—Evil spirit of the Air (in China near Siberia).

Ardad.—A Demon which led travellers astray (East).

Ahriman.—The Spirit of Evil (Persia).

Arma.—Breton fairy.

Arnuphis.—Great Egyptian sorcerer.

Asaphins.—Oniromancers in Chaldea.

Ascaroth.—The Demon of spies and informers.

Asmodeus.—Devil (Hebrew). Asmodeus is said to have tempted Eve.

Asmodel.—The Spirit of the sign of Taurus.

Aspiol.—A kind of evil gnome or spirit.

Asrofil.—The Angel who will announce the Last Judgment (Islam).

Astaroth.—One of the Chief Devils. Astarte is its female.

Auguraculum.—Place where the sacred hens were kept (Rome).

Aulne.—Evil Spirit (Germany).

Avernus.—Pestilential bog at Baiae, said to be the entrance to hell.

Azael.—One of the first angels to rebel. He is said to be chained up until the Last Judgment (Rabbinical legends).

Azariel.—The angel of the waters of the Earth, invoked by fishermen (Talmud).

Angels (Jewish).—Anael, Gabriel, Samael, Michael, Sachiel, Raphael and Camel.

Animals (impure).—Among the Jews, grass-eating animals which do not chew the cud, rabbits and all rodents, pigs, aquatic animals, excepting fishes, flesh-eating birds and water-birds, the ostrich, the bat, the monkey, the lizard and all saurians, batrachians and snakes.

Aziluth.—The Kabbalistic name for the Universe.

B

Baal.—One of the Great Demons (Chaldea).

Bad.—The Spirit of Tempests (Persia).

Bagh.—Magic knot preventing the consummation of marriage (Islam).

Bahaman.—The Spirit of Domestic Animals (Persia).

Bali.—The King of Hell (India).

Banschi.—White lady, Queen of Elves.

Banshee.—Family Spirit (Scotland).

Barbiel.—The Spirit of the sign of Scorpio.

Barcheel.—The Spirit of the sign of Pisces.

Basilisk.—Serpent (born of an egg laid by a toad) whose look killed.

Bechard.—The Demon of Tempests.

Bechet.—The Demon of Friday.

Behemoth.—The Demon of Animal Strength (Hebrew).

Belial.—Demon of the Sidonians.

Beelzebub.—One of the Princes of Hell.

Biergen-Trold.—Spirits of the Woods and Mountains (Faroe Islands).

Bilis.—Madagascan Demon which stops the rice ripening.

Bitabas.—Sudan Sorcerer.

Bithia.—Scythian Witch who bewitched or killed with a look.

Bodilis.—Breton Fountain of Virginity.

Bogle.—Scotch imp.

Bohemians (or Rômes or Gypsies).—According to Papus, low caste Hindus (artisans) who emigrated in mass to Europe.

Bohimum.—Spirit of Evil (Armenia).

Broceliande.—Enchanted Forest in Brittany (Finisterre) where Merlin lives.

Brocken.—General meeting place of German Witches (in the Harz Mountains).

Bucon.—The Demon of Hatred.

Byleth.—One of the Kings of Hell.

Bassantin.—Scotch Astrologer (16th century).

Berson.—Seer at the Court of Henry III of France.
Bonati.—Florentine Astrologer (13th century).
Braccesco.—Italian Alchemist (16th century).
Bragadini.—Italian Alchemist (16th century).

C

Cacomedon.—Evil Spirit. Name given by some Astrologers to the twelfth House.
Caipora.—Gigantic Spirit of the Forests of Brazil. Caiporism belongs to bad luck.
Calchas.—Celebrated soothsayer of Antiquity.
Caliban.—Evil spirit.
Canidia.—Famous sorcerers who cast spells by means of wax dolls.
Caous.—Evil spirits of caves (Caucasus).
Cacoux.—The name of certain malignant ropemakers (Brittany).
Carmenta.—Italian Pythoness.
Chasdins.—Name of Chaldean Sorcerer-Astrologers.
Cheitan.—Arab Demon born of smoke.
Chikk.—Evil Spirit (Arab legends).
Cocles.—Chiromancer of the 16th century.
Couril.—Dwarf spirit with webbed feet which haunts Druidic stones (Brittany, Ireland).
Couropira.—Lame dwarf in Brazilian legends.
Craeteis.—The Goddess of sorcerers and enchanters.
Cumæ.—Old town in Italy celebrated for the grotto where the Sibyl of the same name lived.

D

Demiurg.—According to the Gnosis, the Divine Love to which God has entrusted the management of the World.
Demonology.—The Science of the influence and the nature of Demons.
Demons (Hebrew).—Beelzebub, Samael, Pythin, Asmodeus, Belial, Lucifer and Satan.
Demophila.—The seventh Sibyl of Cumæ, the one who brought the Sibylline books of the Elder Tarquinus.
Dir.—Persian Demon.
Djinn.—A kind of demon or hobgoblin born of flame (East).
Drac.—Familiar spirit, benignant fairy.
Dragon (red).—Book of witchcraft of the 16th century dealing with the art of evoking spirits, making the dead speak, finding hidden treasures, etc.
Drolls.—Northern Demons giving warnings of danger.
Dyonito dal Bergo.—Italian Astrologer (13th century).

E

Elves.—Spirits of Northern Mythology.

Ellivane.—Wandering spirit of Scotch legend.

Eon.—Intermediary between Man and God, according to some Occultists.

Erlking.—The Spirit of Oaks (Germany).

Errohani.—The Magic interpretation of the Koran.

Etraphill.—One of the Moslem angels entrusted with the trumpet of the Last Judgment.

F

Farfadets.—Hobgoblins in Eastern and Scottish legend (not mischievous).

Fires of St. John.—Joy fires to which various superstitions are attached. The night of St. John (24th June) is the shortest and is one of the magic dates of the year. Young girls believed that if on that night they danced nine times round a fire they would soon be married. Sorcerers thought that the night was favourable to the picking of the herbs used in their spells, etc.

Flaga.—Wicked fairy in Scandinavian legend.

Fioraventi.—Alchemist of the 16th century.

G

Gabriel.—Spirit of Aquarius.

Gandreid.—Irish Magic (the power of witches of riding through the air on horse ribs).

Ganga.—Soudanese Magic.

Gauric.—The imp of Megaliths (Brittany).

Geber.—Persian Prince, Sabean author of numerous occult works and chief of the magicians of his time.

Gematry.—In the Kabbala, the study of transpositions.

Genethliacs.—Another name for Astrologers.

Gengues.—Japanese Soothsayers.

Ghaddar.—Arab demon (Upper Egypt).

Ghoul.—The Demon of Graveyards (Arabia).

Goblins.—Spirits of Ships (Brittany).

Gonin.—Old French name for jugglers, snake-charmers, etc.

Goule.—Woman dedicated to the evil spirits.

Gratoulet.—Sorcerer learning to " tie the knot."

Gri-gri.—African Talisman. The most efficacious is a bag containing a piece of the dried navel-string of the wearer.

Guaron.—Another name for the sorcerers of the Middle-Ages.

H

Hamaliel.—The Spirit of the sign of Virgo.
Hanael.—The Spirit of the sign of Capricorn.
Haza.—A Scottish Druidess.
Hexe.—Witch of the North of Europe.
Holda.—A kind of Sabbath (Gaul).
Horei.—Evil Spirit (West Africa).
Huard.—Demon who teases travellers (Brittany).
Hadikin.—Familiar spirit (Anglo-Saxon legend).
Hypophete.—Ancient priest receiving and communicating oracles.

I

Ignis fatuus.—Burning gases arising from certain kinds of soil (containing hydrogen and phosphorus) which our fathers took for spirits or for the souls of the dead.
Incubus.—Male spirit or demon taking a body for the purpose of meeting a woman.
Inescation.—Occult medical process (the transfer of an ill from a man to an animal).
Insemination.—Occult transfer of a human ill into the earth.
Irroration.—Magic healing (by watering plants with the discharge of the patient).
Ithyphallus.—Phallus-shaped amulet.
Iwange.—Sorcerer in the Moluccas.
Iynge.—Kind of love potion.

J

Jakis.—Malignant spirits of the air causing illness (Japan).
Jamambux.—Japanese Fanatics claiming to communicate with the devil.
Jukle.—Spirits of the air (Lapland).
Juripary.—Spirit of Evil (Brazil).

K

Kaho.—A kind of curse (Marquesas Isles).
Kamlat.—Evocation of the Devil by means of a magic drum (Tartars of Siberia).
Kaybora.—Spirit of Woods (America).
Kelpie.—Spirit of Rivers (Scotland).
Kleudde.—Imp (Flanders).
Kobold.—Imp (Ireland).
Koltkis.—Nocturnal spirit (Slavonic legend).
Korrigan.—Dwarf spirit of Druid monuments.

Koughas.—Malignant spirit (Kamtchatka).
Koupai.—Evil spirit (Peru).
Kumacanga.—Name for the werewolf in Brazil.
Kupai.—Name of the Devil (Florida and Peru).
Kircher.—Famous German Jesuit Scientist said to have been a sorcerer (17th century).

L

Ledoux (Miss).—Famous cartomancer (19th century).
Laica.—Good fairy (Peru).
Lamia.—Fabulous spectre with woman's head and serpent's body.
Lanithro.—Demon of the air (Moluccas).
Lase.—Benignant spirit (Thibet).
Lechies.—Female rustic spirits (Slavonic mythology).
Leviathan.—One of the Chief Demons.
Lilith.—Phantom of a cruel beautiful woman (Jewish belief).
Ludlam.—Benign fairy (England).
Laensberg.—Astrologer of Liege (17th century).

M

Magares.—Sorcerers skilled in " tying the knot " (Mingrelia).
Malchichel.—The spirit of the sign of Ram.
Manifest Art.—King of enclyclopædia of kabbalistic signs. Also part of the Kabbala dealing with the science in numbers.
Manitou.—Indian Fetish (North America).
Mantras.—Sanscrit magical formulæ.
Maridh.—Arab demon.
Mastiphal.—One of the Princes of Darkness.
Maty-Tapire.—Lame dwarf of Indian legend.
Mecasphin.—Chaldean sorcerer.
Medrashim.—Kabbalistic books.
Meerman.—Spirit of Water, announcing Tempests (Baltic countries).
Melusine.—Fairy of Poitou (Family spirit of Lusignan).
Meming.—Satyr (Scandinavian Mythology).
Miligma.—Offering to the infernal deities (Greece).
Muhazimim.—Name for possessed persons (Africa).
Muriel.—Spirit of the sign of Cancer.
Mystagogue.—Initiator into Mysteries.
Manto.—Famous pythoness in Thebes.

N

Nakarmkir.—The Spirit of Repentance (Islam).
Narac.—Hell (India).

Nassib.—The Law of Destiny (Turkey).
Nemas.—Malignant spirit (Arabia).
Nidde.—Song of malediction (Scandinavia).
Nirvana.—Buddhistic word denoting the state of the individual losing itself in Nothingness.
Nixes and Nives.—Spirits of water (Germany).
Nornes.—Virgins of Time (Germany).
Notaria.—In the Kabbala, the study of signs.
Nostradamus.—French Astrologer (1503-1566).

O

Oberon.—The King of the spirits of the air (England).
Obi.—Negro sorcerer.
Ombiache.—Madagascar sorcerer.
Ombrophore.—Soothsayer foretelling rain.
Ornen.—The name of the omen given by the augurs.
Orcavelle.—Famous sorceress of romance.
Orias.—Spirit of soothsayers and astrologers.
Ormuz.—The Principle of Good, opposed to Ahriman (Persia).
Orcus.—Old name for Hell.
Ouikka.—Spirit of Evil (Esquimaux).
Ouran.—Magician (East Indies).
Ourisk.—Imp of Scottish legend.
Obereit.—Swiss Alchemist (18th century).
Orenne.—Astrologer (14th century).

P

Pageh.—Indian sorcerer in Brazil.
Pandemonium.—Meeting of Devils. The whole of the Devils.
Paneros.—Fabulous stone relieving barren women.
Patala.—Name of the Indian Hell.
Peri.—Female good spirit (Persia).
Perlimpinpin (powder of).—Made of the ashes of cats, toads, lizards and aspics burnt together. Was used in various " Miracles."
Pctpayaton.—Evil spirit of the air (Siam).
Phylactery.—Amulet made of strips of parchment (Jewish).
Phyleum.—Kind of thistle used in some potions.
Pilla-Karras.—Malabar sorcerer protector of sharks.
Piripis.—Peruvian talisman made of magic plants.
Polyglossos.—Prophetic oak.
Posoera.—Class of witches.
Pousti—Reducing plant used by Fakirs.

Præpates.—Favourable augurs (Roman).
Psychagogy.—Rites for pacifying the Shades.
Psychurgy.—The science of the esoteric principles presiding over birth and death, that is to say the transformations of the soul.
Psylle.—Snake-charmer.

Q

Quirim.—Magic stone which, placed on the forehead of a sleeper, will make him tell what is in his mind.

R

Ranail.—Madagascan spirit.
Rhombus.—Group of sorcerers dancing at the Sabbath.
Runes.—Magic letters used in spells (North of Europe).
Ruggieri.—Florentine Astrologer (16th century).

S

Saalah.—Demon enticing persons into the woods for the purpose of tormenting them (Arab legend).
Sabeism.—Original worship of the stars.
Sacy-Perere.—Cheerful spirit of the Brazilian woods.
Saga, Sagane.—Mediæval names for witches.
Samael.—Spirit of punishments and misfortunes (Persia).
Salutadores.—Healing sorcerers (Spain).
Sanave.—Madagascar amulet.
Schaman.—Sorcerer in Lapland.
Scopelism.—Curse attached to stones thrown into a field or garden.
Senes.—Druidesses of the Island of Sein who calmed the Winds.
Sepher Jesirah.—One of the classic books of the Kabbala.
Sikidy.—Madagascar Astrologer.
Skou.—Spirit of the Woods and Mountains (Faroe Isles)
Soled.—Spirit of the Mountains (Alpine legend).
Sotray.—Imp called Sotret in Lorraine.
Spagyria.—Medical part of Alchemy relating to the composition and decomposition of bodies.
Spir.—Ancient name given to Spirits (hence Spiritism).
Spirits (lower).—These were the gnomes (earth), the undines (water), the imps (air), the salamanders (fire).
Stryge.—Vampire or spectre which ate living beings.
Sulfs.—Name of Sylphs in Gaul (female Sylphid).
Sylphina.—Land of the Sylphs (England, Ireland).
Symmyst.—Person initiated into the Mysteries.
Stadius.—Chiromancer of the time of Henri III of France.

Stoffler.—German Astrologer (15th century).
Swastika.—Buddhist symbol of the Sun, of Light.

T

Taboo.—Objects which may not be touched by any one (New Guinea). Hence the expression, *to be taboo.*
Taconius.—Name of the Fates in Islam.
Taingairi.—Spirits of the air among the Kalmuks.
Talamasc.—Effigy of the Devil exhibited at certain festivals.
Talapoin.—Priest and Magician in Laos.
Talys.—Talisman made of a tiger's tooth (India).
Tamuz.—Name for Hell among the Kalmuks.
Taribot.—Dwarf sorcerer (Madagascar).
Tarni.—Exorcising formula (Kalmuk).
Telet.—Purification rite among the initiates.
Tenebrion.—Spirit of Darkness.
Teraphim.—Automaton's head which foretold the future (Jewish).
Termagaut.—Mediæval idol.
Tervils.—Evil and prophetic demons (Norway).
Teusapoulier.—Malignant spirit inhabiting animals (Brittany).
Themury.—In the Kabbala, the study of commutations and combinations.
Tibalany.—Spectre appearing in trees (Philippines).
Toqui.—Sorcerer (Araucania).
Torngarsuk.—Greenland spirit.
Totem.—Guardian spirit (North America).
Trees (sacred).—The Acacia in Egypt, the Banian in India, the Birch in Kamtchatka, the Oak among the Celts.
Trollen.—Good spirit in Norwegian legend.
Trout which spins.—Lake trout belonging to Gillet-Soulard who was accused of sorcery and burnt in 1466.
Tyre.—Ball of down used in Magic in Lapland.
Tiresias.—Noted soothsayer of Antiquity.

U

Udaci.—Kind of Fakir.
Uphir.—Chemist demon attending to the toilet of Beelzebub.
Utesitura.—Irish magic establishing communication at night with evil spirits.

V

Vaudoisia.—Meeting of Sorcerers (Pays de Vaud, Switzerland).
Verchel.—Spirit of the sign of Leo.

Verdelet.—Demon who carried the Witches to the Sabbath.

Vila.—Spirit of Dalmatian legend.

Vitium.—First word of evil omens.

Verdun.—French sorcerer (16th century).

Villiers (Florent de).—Famous astrologer (15th century).

W

Wairon.—Old name for werewolf.

Watipa.—Malignant spirit of the shore of the Orinoco.

Willis.—White spectres of German legend representing the souls of betrothed women who died before marriage.

Y

Yara.—Kind of siren in Brazil.

Z

Zakum.—Tree in the Mohammedan Hell whose fruits are devil's heads.

Zagam.—Winged demon with bull's head.

Zahuris.—Spanish soothsayers who discover water and hidden treasures (see Magic Rod).

Zohar.—One of the fundamental books of the Kabbala.

Zuriel.—Spirit of the sign of Libra.

THE SWASTIKA

THE FIFTEENTH PLATE OF THE MUTUS LIBER.

This represents the apotheosis of Saturn victor over Jupiter, the solarisation of
the base metal through light and turning into Gold.

Lightning Source UK Ltd.
Milton Keynes UK
UKHW04f0815250918
329438UK00001B/12/P